# The Phonics Handbook

**A handbook for teaching Reading, Writing and Spelling**
**US and Canada edition**

Sue Lloyd

Illustrated by Lib Stephen

Jolly Learning Ltd

UK Edition first published 1992
This US and Canada Edition first published 1993
Second Edition published February 1996

Jolly Learning Ltd
Tailours House
High Road
Chigwell
Essex
IG7 6DL
United Kingdom
Tel: 011 44 181 501 0405
Fax: 011 44 181 500 1696

Printed and bound in England

The blackline masters in this book are in 'Sassoon
Infant', a typeface designed for children learning to read
and write.  The Sassoon typeface are available from
Adobe Systems Inc, 1585 Charleston Road, Mountain
View, CA 94039-7900 Tel: (415) 961 4400

*The  front cover shows two children pretending to be a
donkey, and doing the Sound Sheet action for 'ee' and
'or'.*

*The page numbers in this book have been kept within the
binding, at the base of each page, so that the numbers do
not appear on copies of the reproducible sheets.*

ISBN 1 870946 08 1

# Acknowledgements

My grateful thanks go to Sara Wernham for all her very valuable help and encouragement in producing this book.

I would also like to thank Joan Dorr, Head of Infant Department at Woods Loke Primary School. She took the initiative in encouraging the new thinking in this book, which has resulted in greatly improved results in reading and writing.

I am also very grateful to Dee Corr in Chicago, who first tested these concepts with US teachers, and then edited this book for the US and Canadian market.

# Contents

## PART 2 Reproducible material

# Introduction

This book has been designed to provide a phonic-based system for teaching children to read. Children learn all of the 40+ sounds of the English language, not just the alphabet. They are taken through the stages of blending sounds to form words and then to reading.

The structured, step-by-step approach uses reproducible worksheets and is suitable for a whole school approach and for children in pre-school. Using this method, not only do children learn to read and write more efficiently, but teachers may gain a better understanding of phonics.

The method presented in *The Phonics Handbook* was developed through a series of class-room tested exercises at the Woods Loke Primary School in Lowestoft, Suffolk, England. Before 1975, children at the school were taught to read using a visual, whole word approach. Although most of the children read well, a group of the children had difficulty with reading and writing. These children did not completely understand letter sounds or did not relate these sounds to words. In order to help the children who had problems with reading and writing, the children were taught letter sounds first. The program proved to be a better method of teaching reading to all the children at the school and the group who had problems was much smaller.

In 1977, as part of an experiment, the school introduced structured blending of words to the letter-sounds approach already in use. Children were taught to listen carefully to the sounds in words, to identify the sounds and to relate the sounds to letters. As a result of the experiment, children improved their reading and writing skills and learned to read at an earlier age. Best of all, the group of children with reading problems was almost non-existent. Since then the children at the school have always scored at an average of between 110 and 116 on the Youngs Reading Test, a standardized reading test for children in England. Moreover it has been rare to have a child scoring below 90. (The Youngs Reading Test is so designed that the average score is 100. It is also designed so that half of all children will fall in the range 90-110).

The system presented in *The Phonics Handbook* enables children to identify and blend all the sounds in words before they begin reading words in books. This ground work brings fluency to their reading and writing much earlier.

Our experience over many years, has confirmed the views of others, that visual methods of teaching reading used alone, looking at whole words and sentences and being told what they say, is a poor way to teach reading. We have found that children learn much faster when they know the letter sounds and can work out simple words for themselves before attempting to read whole books. This type of teaching is known as systematic phonic teaching. The alternative is intrinsic phonics which deals incidently with the phonic work. Although intrinsic phonic teaching helps many children, it is not structured and thorough enough for the children with poor auditory ability and memory for words. By teaching in a step by step systematic approach all the children are advantaged. It does not diminish their love of books. On the contrary, the fact that they can actually read the words enhances their pleasure.

Research has shown that systematic phonics results in better word recognition, better spelling, better vocabulary and better reading comprehension[1].

Phonic teaching is a part of the whole teaching process. Comprehension, a wide variety of books and an appreciation of good literature are all important as well, even though they are not covered in this book. This book is designed solely to enable teachers and parents to help their children to understand the mechanics of reading and writing in a structured, systematic and enjoyable way.

[1] Marilyn Jager Adams, Beginning to Read, MIT Press, page 38 for an account of the findings of Chall.

# 1 Sound Sheets.

Children need to be aware that we speak in words and that words are made up of sounds. There are more than 40 sounds in English and 26 letters that are used to represent those sounds. For reading and writing, children must be able to say the sounds that correspond with the letters. The Sound Sheets introduce this concept.

There are 42 letter sounds on the Sound Sheets. (There are 43 letter sounds listed, but c and k are the same letter sound). Each sheet has a suggested storyline, a picture to color, an action, words to read and a line to practice writing the letter(s). Young children are able to learn more quickly when there is an action involved and the more dramatic and exaggerated the action, the more the children will remember. By performing an action for each letter sound, the children are using body movement, ears, eyes and speech to help them remember. This multi-sensory approach is a very effective way of teaching as well as being enjoyable for the children.

## Introducing the Sound Sheets

Using the Sound Sheet for the letter 'm' as an example, you may begin by telling the children a story about going on a picnic in which they are packing their favorite food. As the food is placed in the picnic basket, the children mimic the letter sound by rubbing their stomachs and saying 'mmmmmmmm'. Then ask the children what their favorite food is and also mimic the action for the letter 'm'. After the children learn the action for the letter 'm', you can show them what the letter looks like, and how to write the letter. Ask the children to trace the letter in the air or write it on the chalkboard. A helpful exercise is to have the children look through books and find examples of the letter 'm'. Through this use of the Sound Sheets, children learn that there is a connection between sounds, letters, words and books.

Duplicate copies of the Sound Sheet for the letter 'm' and ask the children to either draw their favorite foods on the plate or cut and paste pictures of their favorite foods on the plate. At the bottom of the sheet, the children can practice writing the letter within the dotted lines, as well as practice the proper pencil grip.

The other letters on the Sound Sheets should be presented in the same manner. It is important to remember that the letter sounds need to be constantly reinforced. The Flash Cards (pages 118 – 132) of the sounds should be used as often as possible since the faster children recognize the sounds, the easier it will be for them to read and write. Once the children have begun to master the sounds they no longer need to do the actions.

When the sound sheets have been completed, the childern can take them home. Parents can be instrumental in developing good learning habits in their children, and they should be encouraged to take an active role in teaching their children to read by practicing the sounds and actions of the letters.

The letters on the Sound Sheets are:

| Page | 43 | a | ..... ants, apple, jam |
| Page | 77 | ai | ..... aim, snail, rain |
| Page | 75 | b | ..... bat, ball, crab |
| Page | 53 | c | ..... cat, clock, duck |
| Page | 63 | d | ..... drum, dog, sad |
| Page | 55 | e | ..... egg, empty, shed |
| Page | 85 | ee | ..... bee, sheep, tree |
| Page | 73 | f | ..... fish, flat, soft |
| Page | 65 | g | ..... gurgle, girl, leg |
| Page | 57 | h | ..... hop, hot, house |
| Page | 47 | i | ..... ink, sit, pin |
| Page | 83 | ie | ..... tie, pie, lie |
| Page | 79 | j | ..... jello, jump, jet |
| Page | 53 | k | ..... kitten, king, kite |
| Page | 71 | l | ..... lollipop, lemon, spell |
| Page | 61 | m | ..... meal, man, summer |
| Page | 51 | n | ..... noise, snap, run |
| Page | 67 | o | ..... on, pond, top |
| Page | 81 | oa | ..... oak, goat, coat |
| Page | 49 | p | ..... pig, puff, top |
| Page | 107 | qu | ..... quack, queen, quick |
| Page | 59 | r | ..... rag, rabbit, forest |
| Page | 41 | s | ..... snake, sun, fast |
| Page | 45 | t | ..... time, top, cat |
| Page | 69 | u | ..... up, umbrella, jump |
| Page | 113 | ue | ..... argue, rescue, barbecue |
| Page | 93 | v | ..... van, vest, drive |

## Letter Sounds

A phonics-based system is successful with children when they are taught, at an early age, to hear and identify the more than 40 sounds in English and to relate these sounds to letters. Although some of the children are slow at first, they can all be trained to hear the sounds in words with proper teaching. This technique is described in the next chapter, 'Auditory Training'.

Teaching the sounds of the alphabet is not enough. If the phonics-based system is to be properly taught, the children need to know all the 40+ sounds, as well as good blending techniques. Consonants are easy for children to understand because there is usually only one sound for each letter. Vowels are more complicated and can be written in several ways. For instance, the 'long a' has three main forms: 'a-e' (came); 'ai' (rain); and 'ay' (stay). In the beginning, it is important that children learn only one way of reading and writing each sound. In this program, the 'ai' is taught first and when the children know this sound they can be taught the 'a-e' and the 'ay'.

## Order of Letter Sound Groups

The letters are arranged in seven, six-letter groups. It is best to follow the recommended order for the seven groups of letters. They have been carefully selected for several reasons. The letters that can be confused, such as 'b' and 'd', are not presented closely together. The 'g' and 'd' come after the 'c' which helps link the formation of the 'c' to the 'd' and 'g'. The first letters taught also combine to make a variety of simple words for the children to blend and read. The Flash Cards, Sound Books, Word Boxes and Letter Games are arranged according to the seven groups to provide an effective systematic approach to teaching children how to read and write.

## Letter Groups

Plan to teach one group each week:
1. s, a, t, i, p, n
2. c k, e, h, r, m, d
3. g, o, u, l, f, b
4. ai, j, oa, ie, ee, or
5. z, w, ng, v, short oo, long oo
6. y, x, ch, sh, voiced th, unvoiced th
7. qu, ou, oi, ue, er, ar

Most children are able to learn six letters a week. It works well to teach two letters on Monday, Wednesday and Friday. It may sound a high target but most children in kindergarten and first grade do achieve this. Although it can be adapted to suit individual needs, we have found a quick introduction works with the majority and then they are free to practice their skills in reading. It should take approximately one hour each day. This leaves an hour on Tuesday and Thursday for revision and playing letter games. The children like going into a story corner with the letters. One child pretends to be the teacher, holds up the letters and the others do the action sounds.

In the Reproducible Section 6 (pages 166-174), are the Matching Letters, Words and Pictures. They can be used by putting out the pictures from the sheets and having the children put the initial letters under them.

In the Reproducible Section 11 (pages 203-212), the Letter Games include 'Lotto' and 'Pairs', which can help the children gain fluency by saying the letter sounds.

## Sound Books

You can encourage the children to practice the sounds of the letters by helping them create their own sound book. This could be a plain exercise book that you have cut horizontally in half. Once you have taught the children a letter, paste the letter on the next clean page and gradually each child will have their own book of all the letter sounds. You also can have the children take the book home each night and encourage their parents to practice the sounds in their books. You can encourage the children by rewarding them with a star when they 'read' their books well.

## *Supplementary Work*

In most classes, there will be a few children who are not learning the sounds as quickly as the other children. There are three main reasons for this:

1.  The child has a poor memory for letters and words.
2.  There is no parental help or co-operation.
3.  The child's attendance at school is poor or limited in some way.

One way to overcome this problem would be to determine which letter sounds the child does not know and put those letters in a box for the child to take home with the Sound Book. Gradually, the letters the child does not know can be added to the box. These children need plenty of praise and encouragement. It is important that you explain to the parents that their child needs extra support and ask for their assistance.

You can also help children by inviting interested parents to come to the classroom and play the games 'Lotto' and 'Pairs' (pages 203-207) with the children who need more practice saying the sounds. Another good game for a parent to play, with two children who are not yet proficient with the sounds, is to sit between them and turn over the letters. The first child to say the sound can be given the letter, and the one who receives the most letters wins. Another aid that the children can use is an audio card reader such as the Language Master. The audio card can have a letter sound recorded on it by the teacher, and have the letter(s) written on the card. The children attempt to say the sound first, before pushing the card through the machine, and hearing correctly. It requires little teacher time and is self correcting. It can also be used for reading words, consonant blends, ways of writing vowels and reading irregular words.

## Conclusion

By concentrating on the letters before asking the children to read books for themselves, most children are soon able to learn the more than 40 sounds of English and the letters that make those sounds.

However, just learning the letter sounds is not enough. The children also need to know how to apply this knowledge. The children should also be taught to blend the sounds and hear the words. It is a technique that *can* be taught and is covered in the next chapter.

# 2 Auditory Training

## Auditory skills for reading

Literate adults are so fluent at reading and writing that we fail to realize how much we use our ears. For example, when someone tells you the name of a city you are unfamiliar with, such as Manitowoc, you listen for the sounds and try to think of the letters that would go with the sounds. You would confidently predict that 'Manitowoc' begins with 'Man', then expect 'i', and 'to' or 'toe', finishing with 'woc' or 'wock'. All the time you listen first and then try to apply your letter knowledge. In this program, the children are given this understanding at an early age, which is the main reason for the program's success in teaching reading and writing.

As early as the first day of school, it is possible to determine which children have a natural ability to hear the sounds in words. You may say to the children, "I want you to listen very carefully because I am going to say sounds and you may be able to hear a word. If you can hear it, say it out loud .... D-O-G." Invariably, at least one child will hear the word 'dog' and say it aloud. This child has good auditory ability. If the children do not hear it, tell them the word and try a different three-letter word. By repeating the process, you will see that more children will be able to hear the words. Keep to short words in the beginning, and do a little auditory work every day.

After two weeks most children know at least the first six letter sounds. You can then write three-letter words, such as tap, pan, sit and pin, on the chalkboard or on individual cards to show the children. The children who can hear the words understand how reading works and they realize that it is something they can do by themselves. This knowledge fascinates them and their confidence in their own ability grows.

# Blending Sounds

Blending is simply the action of running the letter sounds together to make a word. Literate adults are skillful at blending. When we see or hear an unfamiliar word, we say the sounds that usually go with the letters in that word. Although we do not always pronounce the word properly, we do use our experience with words and letters to choose a pronunciation that we believe is correct. In doing so, we are blending sounds together.

There are two reasons for children being unable to hear the words when they have said the sounds:

1.   They do not know the sounds well enough. As soon as they see a letter, the sound should come automatically to them. If they delay, they lose track of the word. To correct this, you have to play more letter games and do regular flash card work.

2.   The letter sounds are not emphasized correctly. Children must learn to say the first letter sound loudly and whisper the others fluently, for example, **d**-o-g and **h**-a-t. With the correct technique and daily practice, children will ultimately be successful.

## Word Box Sheets

Before the children start reading books, they should practice blending letter sounds to form words. In Reproducible Section 4 (pages 141-154), you will find sheets with words that are suitable for Word Boxes. These pages can be copied, and pasted on tagboard, and then cut into individual word cards. It is recommended that two sets of each page be made. The pages could also be laminated for greater durability. The cards should be stored in boxes or zip-lock plastic bags and labeled Word Box (or bag) 1, Word Box (or bag) 2, etc. After the fifth of the letter groups has been taught, allow the children to take the cards home on a rotating basis to practice the sounds and words with their parents.

Choose the two children who are best at blending and give them Word Box (or bag) 1. The children could read the words aloud the next day to you or a helper. The words do not need to be learnt by heart, because it is a blending exercise. Some children will read the words without blending. These children have a good visual memory for words and they should be encouraged to continue reading the words straight away. If the children read their words confidently, whether they blend or not, give them Word Box 2, and give Word Box 1 to the next group of children who are doing well with blending. Most children should be given a new box each day. This exercise can take about three to four weeks to complete.

## Supplementary Work

The children who have problems blending need supplementary work. If they have difficulty blending because they do not know the letter sounds, they should not be given the Word Boxes, but rather practice the letters until they are fluent at saying the sounds. However, if the children do know the letter sounds well, but still find it difficult to hear the word, let them use a box of words. If necessary, reduce the number of words in the box and gradually give them the supplementary words (listed on page 142). They may have to use the box for more than one day. Gradually, they should improve their blending.

# Identifying the sounds in words

In reading, the auditory skill needed is the ability to perceive the word after having recognised the sounds. With writing, on the other hand, we need to be able to hear, identify and write the sounds of a word. For example, in the word 'bin', you listen and hear the 'b..i..n'. If you know how to write those letters, you can write the word 'bin' without help.

To begin with, this auditory work should be just to help reading. The children try to hear the word sounded out by you. After that, the children will need the auditory skills for writing. You should choose a three-letter word, preferably made up of the letters that they have learned such as 'pin'. Ask the children what sound they can hear at the beginning. Usually they get the 'p' because the initial letter is the easiest to identify. Then they should try to get the other two letters. The letters that they have already learned should be on display. The children should select the letters as they are identified, and lay them out in the correct order to form the word. When children can pick out the sounds in a word, they understand how writing works.

To speed up the auditory work, you should teach the children to say the sounds quickly for the two- or three-letter words you say aloud. As they say each sound, they should hold up a finger for each sound. Do several of these exercises each day using words such as pet, hat, wet, in, leg and bed. The exercise takes only a few minutes to complete.

When the children can sound out three-letter words, you can progress to longer words. This often involves hearing the consonant blends.

### Initial Consonant Blends

bl, cl, fl, gl, pl, sl, br, cr, dr, dw, fr, gr, pr, tr, sc, sk, sm, sn, sw, tw, scr, spl, spr, st and str.

### Final Consonant Blends

lb, ld, lf, lk, lm, ln, lp, lt, ct, ft, nt, pt, xt, mp and nd.

It is important that the children hear the individual sounds in the consonant blends. To develop this, you should say the blends, for example, 'cr' and the children should say 'c..r', putting up a finger for each sound. Repeat a few examples each day and gradually the children will become fluent at identifying the sounds in the consonant blends. The following list is helpful to refer to for words containing initial and final consonant blends:

| | | | | | |
|---|---|---|---|---|---|
| bran | clap | clip | club | flag | flat |
| flap | flip | glad | plan | plug | plum |
| plot | slap | slim | slug | crab | crop |
| drag | drip | drop | drug | drum | frog |
| from | grab | grim | grip | print | prop |
| trim | trap | trip | scan | smog | smart |
| snap | snip | snug | swam | swim | swum |
| twig | twin | bulb | held | golf | milk |
| silk | film | help | gulp | belt | melt |
| quilt | gift | lift | soft | ant | pant |
| bent | went | tent | mint | hunt | kept |
| next | camp | damp | lamp | limp | bump |
| jump | lump | band | land | bend | mend |
| wind | pond | skip | desk | spin | step |
| best | nest | lost | must | plump | slept |
| frost | grand | crisp | | | |

After the consonant blends, you should progress to the point where you can call out any word, including long words, and the children should be able to identify all the sounds in the words. For example:

splendid — s.p.l.e.n.d.i.d — 8 fingers up, 8 sounds in the word.
ground — g.r.ou.n.d — 5 fingers up, 5 sounds.
crumble — c.r.u.m.b.le — 6 fingers up, 6 sounds.
shoot — sh.oo.t — 3 fingers up, 3 sounds.

Gradually, the children become accustomed to hearing all the sounds and understand that some sounds are represented by two or more letters. Hearing sounds such as 'n' in 'dent' and the 'er' in 'dinner' are usually the most difficult. The children who have difficulty hearing the sounds may lose the skill if they are not supervised. These children need regular practice. Through their writing, you can determine how well they are hearing the sounds. For example, if they write 'sped' for 'spend', you know they need more auditory training.

Other ways of encouraging children to listen to the sounds in words are nursery rhymes, and through these activities:

1. Word Families (see Reproducible Section 7, pages 175-179)

2. Hear the word after the initial sound has gone.

   | *Teacher says* | | *Children respond* |
   |---|---|---|
   | pink | ............ | ink |
   | mice | ............ | ice |
   | bus | ............... | us |
   | block | ............ | lock |
   | twin | ............ | win |

3. Finish the word. The teacher says whole word, such as split, and then breaks it down getting the children to finish the word. For example: s...plit, sp...lit, spl...it, spli...t.

4. Hear the number of syllables. The teacher says a word and the children tap out the number of syllables.

Most adults know the sounds of the letters of the alphabet, but if they are asked what the more than 40 sounds of the English language are, they probably would struggle to get some of them. Generally, they are not familiar with the following:

| | | |
|---|---|---|
| Short oo | ...... | (book) |
| Long oo | ...... | (moon) |
| ar | ...... | (car) |
| er, ir, ur | ...... | (father, bird, burn) |
| or, au, aw, al | ...... | (port, auction, awful, talk) |
| oi, oy | ...... | (boil, boy) |
| ou, ow | ...... | (out, owl) |
| ng, nk | ...... | (song, sink) |
| y as a vowel | ...... | (funny, fly) |

## Supplementary Work

Most children will learn to hear the sounds in words during class auditory training. The few who are finding it difficult need to be taught in the same manner, but in a group of their own or, if possible, individually.

## Some Key Points

The program outlined has three key components:

1. Awareness of the 40+ letter sounds of English.
2. Ability to blend these sounds to form words (so as to read).
3. Ability to identify the sounds in words, and relate these sounds to the letters (so as to write).

The development of these abilities is essential to the teaching of reading and writing.

# 3 Reading Books

## Pre-reading skills

At this point, the children should know the letters that usually go with the more than 40 sounds (Chapter 1), and they should be able to blend letter sounds in simple words and hear the words (Chapter 2).

The children will also need to learn irregular sight words such as 'was', 'they', 'the' and 'you'. The words should be put on flash cards and used regularly for review. Some of the most commonly used irregular words are:

| | | | | | |
|---|---|---|---|---|---|
| of | to | was | you | one | said |
| they | some | come | once | do | could |
| should | would | other | mother | brother | there |
| where | who | what | their | two | want |

When most of the children know the letter sounds well and have read the 'blending practice words' in the Word Boxes, they are ready to read books independently. In the beginning, it is best to use a reading series since children gain confidence when the vocabulary in the books increases gradually. For those children whose word memory is not good, the controlled vocabulary is particularly important. As soon as the children are reading confidently, they can choose trade books that are not in the reading series.

Up to now, the children are likely to have read only phonically regular words. You can now tell them that there are some irregular words which are more difficult to sound out. Pick out the irregular words from the beginning books in the reading series you are going to use, or from the preceding list. By looking at words, and discussing the irregularities of words, the children become familiar with them. For example, you could show them the word 'said' and see if they can tell you the irregular part. The letters 'ai' do not make a long 'ai' sound (as in maid) but a short 'e' sound (as in 'bed'). Children can be shown how words are built, which will create a greater awareness of how words are spelled. There are some words such as 'one', 'once', 'could', 'ought' and 'laugh', that cannot be sounded. Tell the children that these irregular words must be memorized. At times the children will find a word in their reading books they can almost read and, if they think about the context, they can often successfully figure it out.

Children often become excited when they receive their first reader. They have worked hard learning how to read and now they are putting what they learned into practice. It is helpful, in the beginning, if parents and teachers listen to the children reading every day. You could write the number of pages that you want a child to read on a reading card. Five pages is a good starting number. Parents can be asked to cross off the numbers on the reading card as the child reads the pages. However, if the child only wants to read one page, the parents could note this on the card. On the other hand, if the child wants to finish a story, the child should be allowed to do so and the parents can note the number of pages the child has read. The parents can ask their child to try to figure out unfamiliar words by blending the letter sounds together. You could also ask the parents to talk about the story with their child, in order to increase the child's comprehension skills.

When a child is reading fluently and being supported by his/her parents, you only need to ask a little about the story, exchange the book and then once a week make sure the reading is satisfactory. Although a child might be able to read the words in a book, it is extremely important that he/she understands and enjoys the book. For example, a child may be able to read the words in a Charles Dickens' book, but he or she would not understand the content of the book. If reading is fluent but comprehension is not good, the child should be given a book with less complex sentence structure and story line.

After the children have been reading aloud, it is advisable to introduce silent reading for ten minutes a day. During the silent reading time, you can go to all the children and see how much they have read the previous night. A check mark on the reading card and an encouraging word will keep their enthusiasm high and develop the habit of reading every night. It also makes you aware of the children who have not had help at home.

## Supplementary Work

By the end of the semester, most children will have gone through the boxes of words for blending and will be reading books. Children who are still unable to read may have a poor visual memory for letter sounds and words. It is likely they also have poor blending techniques and auditory ability. These children can be encouraged to play games that will improve their knowledge of letter sounds, such as the games in Reproducible Section 11 (pages 203-212), as well as practicing the blending of small words. They need praise and encouragement for what they do know and should be taught at their own pace. These children may be the only ones without a reading book, and it may be psychologically better for them to have a book, even if their pre-reading skills have not been completely mastered. However, it is still important to keep reviewing letter sounds and blending simple words because this is the only way they will be able to make real progress.

Occasionally a child will read by sounding aloud every letter of each word and should be taught to blend words silently. If a child is too hesitant about reading a page aloud, it is better to have him/her practice reading that page again. At this stage the enjoyment comes from mastering the skills of reading and, as the fluency increases, the story itself becomes the most enjoyable part of reading.

If children find it difficult to recognize the different sounds of the vowels, such as 'mad' (short a) and 'made' (long a), encourage them to try sounding the word out using the short vowel first and if that does not fit into the context of the story, try the long vowel.

## Some Key Points

1.  The pre-reading skills taught during the first semester help children figure out simple words. They will be better prepared when they come to reading books for themselves.

2.  In the early stages of reading, it is best to use a reading series with controlled vocabulary. When the children are reading fluently, they can choose trade books for independent reading.

3.  The children should be encouraged to talk about the story they have read to ensure they have good comprehension.

# 4 Writing

Independent writing develops much quicker when children are able to sound out words and write the letters for those sounds. By listening to letter sounds, they can write the words they hear and not just the words they have memorized.

Children are helped in this activity by watching you demonstrate the technique first. You may want to use an easel board in the story corner so the children are close to your examples and can sometimes write the words on the board. In the first stage, say simple phonically regular words such as leg, hop, hat and cup. The children say the sounds in the words, and you write the letters for those sounds on the board.

Parents can be very helpful at this stage, since most parents are willing to say words for their children to write. These words are on the Homework Writing Sheets in Reproducible Section 5 (pages 155-165). As soon as children have the auditory ability to identify the sounds in simple words and the manipulative skill to write the letters, they can start on the Homework Writing Sheets.

## Homework Writing Sheets

Each Homework Writing Sheet is divided into six groups of words. Make a copy of the first Homework Writing Sheet for each child and put the child's name in the top right-hand corner. Then, as you cut off each set of ten words, you know which sets the child still has to do. Cut off one of these sets of ten words and put it into each child's Homework Writing Book. These books can be made by cutting a wide lined exercise book vertically in half (the loose sheets that are cut off can be used for writing words in class), or by stapling together half-sheets of wide-lined manuscript paper. Include one of the Instruction Strips for Parents (page 165), in each child's Homework Writing Book.

When the homework is returned, cut off the next set of words from the child's sheet and send it home in the homework book. It is not necessary for the child to have every word correct before being given the next set of words. However, if time permits, point out what mistakes have been made. The majority of children can do this every night, although it is not essential. It is important that parents understand that the words are for them to say, and not simply for the children to copy.

The correct formation of every letter is given at the base of each Sound Sheet. Parents should be asked to watch their children as they write and correct any wrong formation.

Gradually, as the children progress through the writing sheets, the words become more difficult. By the time they have completed all the homework sheets, they should be able to listen for sounds and write phonically regular words.

## Classroom Activities

The fact that writing is a way of communicating needs to be explained to the children. Many teachers start this by asking each child to draw a picture of something that happened recently. After the picture has been drawn, the children talk about it and the teacher writes one of their sentences under the picture. It is a good way to show children that their thoughts can be put down in print. For teachers following this program, the letters should be sounded out for most of the words. For example, if the child wants you to write, "We went for a picnic in the woods", as you write the sentence, you should be breaking the words up and show how they are made of sounds by saying "W.e w.e.n.t f.or a p.i.c.n.i.c i.n th.e w.oo.d.s". Skip over irregular words and put emphasis on sounding the regular words. Some adults are unable to sound out words at first because they are accustomed to writing automatically from memory and find it difficult to break familiar words up into their sound values. Once you have done this sounding out a few times, it becomes easier.

In the beginning teachers should not ask children to copy under the teacher's writing. Correct letter formation is important from the start. If children copy letters before they have been shown how to form them, bad writing habits are likely to result.

## *Classroom Worksheets*

The Classroom Worksheets in Reproducible Sections 6-10 (pages 166-202) have been designed to encourage the children to read and write independently. For reading, the children put words under pictures or join them with a line. With the writing, the children have to fill in the missing sound or write all the sounds. They look at the picture to get the word, and then write the missing sounds in that word. The pictures can be colored and the sheet taken home.

## *Supplementary Work*

If children do not do their writing homework, it is important that they practice by writing words dictated in school using one of the following methods.

1.  Ask an interested parent to come into the classroom and help the child by dictating the words. This is the best help because the parent can make a note of any problems the child has. For example: 'He/she does not know how to write the letter 'f' or 'He/she could not hear the final sound in a word'.

2.  Ask a child who is good at reading to read aloud the words on the Homework Writing Sheets for the child to write.

3.  Take a small group of children yourself and read the words aloud. This can be done when the other children in the classroom are busy with other activities, such as a Classroom Worksheet.

4.  Use a tape recorder with the method described in Chapter 5 on Spelling (page 30).

# *Independent Writing*

When the children have completed the Homework Writing Sheets, they should be able to write words on their own. By using the Classroom Worksheets in class, they will be accustomed to figuring out words and finishing a written sentence. Children need to write a complete sentence by themselves, and a good way to begin is by asking them to tell about something that happened recently. Instead of writing one of the sentences for them, encourage them to write about it. Remind them to listen for the sounds in each word and write the letters for those sounds. The fact that words are not spelled correctly is not a concern during beginning writing activities. Most children eventually spell words correctly because they see the words many times in their reading books. Recent research has shown that when children start writing by sounding out words before they have learned to spell them, they later become better at spelling. The same research also showed that they were better at reading and composition.

The advantages of learning to write by sounding out words are considerable – children can express themselves in writing without help at an earlier age, they can write exactly what they want to say, and they use a larger vocabulary because they are not limited to the words they can spell. They also become better at spelling because they are continually aware of the sounds in words and the letter patterns that are linked to the sounds. The confidence they gain from being independent writers encourages them to write more, and the more they write, the better they become.

Most children should be able to write a page of three to five sentences by the end of the first year. The children who have a good visual memory for words will always find it much easier to spell correctly. However, in order to achieve high standards, it is important that all children participate in a structured spelling program. This is covered in Chapter 5, Spelling.

Most vowel sounds have several ways of being written. Using the example given earlier, the long 'a' sound is usually written as 'ai' (rain), 'a-e' (late) or 'ay' (day). As soon as the children know the letter sounds well, it is important to teach the vowel digraphs in which two letters make a single sound.

When the children want to write a word like 'late', they know it starts with 'l' and then a long 'a' sound. The children should be taught that it is not likely to be 'ay' because that sound usually comes at the end of words. The last sound is 't', so the word is either written 'lait' or 'late'. Often the children, especially if they have a good visual memory, will choose the correct one because they have seen it written in books.

The following list gives the main alternative ways of writing the vowels and these should be taught first. Later, more variations can be taught so that gradually the children build up their phonics skills.

*Vowel sound*

| | |
|---|---|
| long a | ai, a-e, ay (chain, late, day) |
| long e | ee, ea (sleep, dream) |
| long i | ie, i-e, igh, y (pie, ride, light, fry) |
| long o | oa, o-e, ow (coat, bone, snow) |
| long u | ue, u-e, ew (Tuesday, cute, few) |
| short oo | oo, u (book, put) |
| long oo | oo, u-e, ue, ew (moon, rude, blue, chew) |
| ar sound | ar, a (barn, father) |
| er sound | er, ir, ur (summer, girl, burn) |
| or sound | or, au, aw, al (sport, auction, awful, talk) |
| oi sound | oi, oy (boil, toy) |
| ou sound | ou, ow (out, brown) |

The child's awareness of the sounds in words and knowledge of the letters that usually go with those sounds enables reading and writing to develop more easily. By the end of their second year, most children will be above average on standardized spelling tests.

Children become quite fascinated at the analytical approach to looking at words. They start looking in their reading books and finding the different ways of writing vowel sounds, and gradually they learn the alternative ways of writing them. You can suggest to the children that if they are not sure how to write a word, they should write the alternative ways on scrap paper. Often they will pick out the correct spelling because it looks right and they remember it from their reading.

It is important that children know there is a correct way to spell every word. When they start writing by themselves it is impossible to spell correctly all the words they want to use, however, they must be taught that before they write a word they should think how to spell it. If they do not know the word, they should write the sounds they can hear so that their writing is at least phonically correct.

When children first start writing, they only think in sounds, but gradually, they become accustomed to thinking of the sounds and correct spelling as they write. By the end of the second year, most children are writing automatically and are able to concentrate on correct spelling.

## Supplementary Work

Generally, children who are slower at learning to read tend to take longer to master independent writing. In order to help them, you must first diagnose their problem.

It might be one of the following:

1.  The child can hear the sounds but cannot remember how to write the letters for the sounds. It would appear that remembering how to write letters is a different process from recognizing them in print. To correct this, first find out which letters are not known and ask parents or other children to dictate them to the child so the child can write them. Even a child with a poor memory will master this fairly quickly with extra practice. When independent writing is being attempted, it is helpful if they have all 42 letter sounds written on a card, and if they cannot remember how to write the letters they can refer to the card.

2.  The child knows the letter sounds and can identify the sounds in words but has poor physical pencil control. In this case the child can be given fine motor control exercises, coloring pictures and drawing patterns. Until the pencil control skills develop, you can write what the child wants to say making sure the child sounds out most of the words.

3. The child cannot hear the sounds in the words. Without the skill to hear and identify the sounds, it is impossible for the child to write independently. It is important to continue with the auditory training in Chapter 2 and to make sure the child knows how to write the letters when you say the sounds. This child will benefit from doing the supplementary Homework Writing Sheets in Reproducible Section 5 (listed on page 156) and the full set of worksheets with missing sounds and words in Reproducible Section 8 (pages 180-190). All children can be tuned into hearing the sounds in words. However, some children need more time and practice.

For children who are naturally good at writing the sounds in words and reading, there are Advanced Homework Writing Sheets (Reproducible Section 5). These cover the various ways of writing the vowels and are a challenge to those children who have a good memory for words.

## Some Key Points

1. When children are taught to hear and identify the sounds in words and are shown the letters that usually go with those sounds, they can write independently at an earlier age.

2. When children learn to write by sounding out words first, as opposed to trying to remember how to spell words, they become better at spelling.

3. Children who have been taught to write by listening to the sounds use a wider vocabulary in their writing.

# 5 Spelling

The ability to spell accurately is directly related to the memory for words and the phonic letter understanding that has been acquired. When children have been taught to listen and identify the sounds in words and know the different ways of writing those sounds, they have a good phonic understanding. From then on, it is necessary to review the letter sound knowledge and develop spelling strategies to help the children remember the words.

The program outlined so far covers the first year of school when children are taught to read and write independently by sounding out words. Usually, there is not enough time to introduce a systematic spelling program as well. However, there are a few things that need to be covered before the children start the spelling program in their second year:

1.  The first step would be to teach the names of the 26 letters of the alphabet for those children who have begun school without knowing the alphabet. Young children like to sing the alphabet and it is an easy way for them to learn it. The more familiar the children are with the letter sequence in the alphabet, the easier it is to use a dictionary. To help them learn letter sequence, mix up a set of alphabet letters and ask the children to put them in the correct order. When they are proficient at this, you can time the activity and challenge the children to put the letters in sequence as quickly as possible. Regular practice in looking up words in simple dictionaries should be encouraged as soon as the children are reading confidently.

2.  The children should be taught to recite the short and long vowels ... a−e−i−o−u and know that 'y' can sometimes be a vowel such as in the words 'sky' and 'my'. This knowledge is useful when they are learning spelling patterns later on. Once the children know the vowels, they can be told that all the other letters in the alphabet are called consonants.

3.  Capital letters should be introduced at the same time that the Sound Sheets are being used. The children should be told that these letters are used in certain places such as at the beginning of names, days of the week and months. It is some-

times difficult for young children to know where a sentence ends, so it is equally difficult for them to cope with a capital letter at the beginning of a sentence. Talk with the children about the periods that are at the end of each sentence in their readers and note that each new sentence begins with a capital letter.

## Spelling Program

Children should be taught the 'LOOK, COVER, WRITE and CHECK' way of learning to spell. The children should be asked to look carefully at the word they want to learn and to note what is different about it. For example, in the word 'said', it is the middle letters that sound wrong because the sound in the middle is a short 'e' and not a long 'a'. After the children have carefully looked at the word, they cover the word and write it. As soon as they have written the word, they check to see they have written it correctly. They repeat the process until they have written the word correctly three times.

When we write, there are certain words that are used often. Some of these high frequency words are irregular in the way they are spelled, and should be the first words on which to concentrate.

**High Frequency Words:**

| | | | | | |
|---|---|---|---|---|---|
| he | came | our | gave | saw | egg |
| she | come | over | girl | say | hill |
| me | some | other | give | school | horse |
| we | could | mother | going | take | letter |
| be | would | brother | green | tell | milk |
| of | should | another | head | these | money |
| to | do | any | home | think | morning |
| was | go | away | house | three | name |
| all | no | because | how | time | night |
| are | first | bird | keep | too | nothing |
| for | her | black | know | tree | picture |
| have | here | blue | last | under | place |
| one | into | boy | live | walk | rabbit |
| said | like | day | many | white | road |
| so | little | every | May | why | sea |
| they | look | eat | Mr. | work | sister |
| you | book | very | Mrs. | woman | street |
| about | made | fast | once | year | table |

| | | | | | |
|---|---|---|---|---|---|
| back | make | father | next | bush | tea |
| been | more | fell | open | apple | today |
| before | down | find | own | children | toy |
| by | new | five | play | cow | train |
| my | now | fly | put | dinner | water |
| call | off | four | read | doll | cousin |
| ball | only | found | round | door | Grandfather |

Start the spelling program by introducing five of these high frequency words. The children can practice writing these words with the 'LOOK, COVER, WRITE and CHECK' method. Then ask the children to write the words neatly on a piece of paper to take home. Check the spelling of the words to be sure the children have copied the words correctly. Parents should be asked to help their children learn these words, and then, after a few days, to test the children on the spelling of these words. After you have done this for a few sets of five words, one set each week, you will be able to identify the children who are having trouble and who are not able to learn at the pace of the other children. These children will follow a slightly different program, which is explained in this Chapter's Supplementary Work section.

The majority of children have no difficulty in learning five words a week. This can be gradually increased to ten words. One suggestion would be to have the children copy the words on Friday and practice the words at home over the weekend. They should ask their parents to read the words to them so they can learn them. On Monday, or later in the week, you can give the children a spelling test on these words. They should be praised for their efforts and improvement in spelling correctly.

After the list of high frequency words has been mastered, you can develop your own spelling program. Some teachers like to use words relating to a topic or subject being taught, others use categories such as vegetables or days of the week while other teachers prefer to use a published spelling word list.

A useful technique for learning certain irregular words is to teach all the children to say the word in the way suggested by the spelling. For example with the word 'mother' ... instead of saying it as 'muther', the children say 'mother' with a short 'o' being used (to rhyme with 'bother'). It goes like this:

| Teacher says | Children respond |
|---|---|
| mother | mother (to rhyme with bother) |
| put | put (to rhyme with but) |
| was | was (to rhyme with gas) |
| Monday | Mon day |
| Wednesday | Wed nes day |
| February | Feb ru ary |

The children quickly understand that they are saying the words incorrectly, in order to help them remember the irregular spellings. It does not affect the use of these words in their normal conversation. Start by calling out just a few of these words. Later repeat them and as the response from the children becomes well known, then add more to the list. It is the kind of activity you can do while the children are changing for games. The following list has a few more examples:

| | | | | |
|---|---|---|---|---|
| push | pull | pudding | December | once |
| one | two | want | do | go |
| no | other | brother | another | front |
| oven | friend | pretty | knife | know |
| knight | write | wrong | lamb | could – c ou ld |

## Correcting the Spelling of Independent Writing

Children following this program start writing by sounding out words and writing the letters they think go with those sounds. Consequently, many words are spelled incorrectly. Young children could become discouraged if their independent writing papers were covered with red correction marks. Rather, they should be praised for their writing, and, if words have been written with a wrong or missing sound, this should be pointed out and corrected. For example, if he or she writes the word 'went' as 'wet', ask the child to sound out the word he or she has written. The child will soon realize that he or she has written 'wet' and by listening carefully can hear that the 'n' sound is missing.

In second grade the words that have been taught already in the program should be corrected if misspelled. It is better to correct three or four words at a time and ask the children to practice these with the 'LOOK, COVER, WRITE and CHECK' technique. If you correct more than four misspellings at a time, the children could become discouraged and perhaps dislike independent writing. If they make a phonic mistake that you think they should know, it is necessary to point it out. For example, if they write 'cam' for 'came', they need to be reminded that the long 'a' needs the 'e' at the end of the word.

As the children continue on with independent writing, they need an indication of errors. Correct the words the children should know and put a dot beneath the error in each misspelled word they would not be expected to know. This lets them know there is an error, but it is not a serious one.

By the time they are eight years old, they should be able to spell correctly most of their everyday words. Good spellers usually know if they cannot spell a word, and these children should be encouraged to write the different spelling alternatives on scrap paper. If they are still unsure of the word, they should look it up in a dictionary. Encourage the children who are having problems to continue to sound out unknown words to keep the flow of their writing. They can learn to spell the incorrect words later.

## Supplementary Work

Children who are having spelling difficulties need special help. They should watch and listen with the other children when you are talking about the words the other children are to take home to learn and any phonics rules you are explaining. When the other children write their lists of words to take home, these children should have their own shorter lists.

They need to learn in small chunks with a lot of repetition, and should learn a few words and keep practicing these words on a daily basis as new words are added. To achieve this effectively in the classroom a tape recorder can be used. If it is impossible to have a tape recorder, pair the children up and get them to take turns in saying and spelling the words with their partners.

## Tape Recorder Spelling

On a tape, record the first four frequently used words. Say each word twice as clearly as possible. Sometimes you may have to use the target word in context. For example, 'Two − it is the number two'. The child listens to the word, stops the tape, writes the word and then restarts the tape. He or she continues until all the words are written. Put a list of the children who are to use the tape next to the tape recorder so when each child has written the words, he or she can cross off his or her name and then allow the next child to use the tape recorder. When you have checked their work, any words that are wrong should be practiced using the 'LOOK, COVER, WRITE and CHECK' technique. The children should take the list of words home for more practice. The next day they write the same four words from the tape and see if they have spelled them correctly.

The following week, record four new words following the original four on the tape. The children will then write the eight words every day. In doing so, they are getting the repetition of the first set of words and starting to learn the next set. The third week, record another four words, which increases the total to 12 words. The children continue listening to the tape and writing the words every day. By the fourth week, the children should know the first four words and these words can be erased from the tape and four new ones added. This means that they never write more than twelve words at a time and they repeatedly practice each word every day for three weeks. A chart which records the children's progress encourages their efforts.

**Example for starting the words on a tape recorder**
(taken from the list of High Frequency Words, page 26)

| First Week | Second Week | Third Week | Fourth Week |
|------------|-------------|------------|-------------|
| he | he | he | be |
| she | she | she | of |
| me | me | me | to |
| we | we | we | was |
|  | be | be | all |
|  | of | of | are |
|  | to | to | for |
|  | was | was | have |
|  |  | all | one |
|  |  | are | said |
|  |  | for | so |
|  |  | have | they |

You can also test the children's phonic knowledge using the tape recorder by asking them to:

1. write the two 'ou's …………………answer: ou, ow
2. write the two 'oi's …………………answer: oi, oy
3. write the three main 'ai's …………answer: ai, a-e, ay
4. write the two main 'ee's …………answer: ee, ea
5. write the four main 'ie's …………answer: ie, i-e, igh, y

6. write the three main 'oa's ............answer: oa, o-e, ow
7. write the three main 'ue's ............answer: ue, u-e, ew
8. write the 'ng' sound ....................answer: ng
9. write the 'nk' sound ....................answer: nk
10. write the 'ar' sound's ................answer: ar
11. write the three main 'er's ...........answer: er, ir, ur
12. write the four main 'or's ..............answer: or, au, aw, al
13. write the two main short 'oo's ......answer: oo, u
14. write the four main long 'oo's ........answer: oo, u-e, ue, ew

## Some Key Points

1. Children with a good memory for words and the ability to relate sounds in words to letters, learn to spell accurately with relative ease.

2. Children start independent writing much earlier and use a wider vocabulary when they identify the sounds in words and write the letters for those sounds.

3. Children who are experiencing spelling difficulties need a systematic spelling program that has sufficient repetition to bring success. They also need to listen for the sounds and relate them to their letter knowledge.

### Further phonic knowledge

*The Phonics Handbook* is designed to help schools, teachers and students teach reading with a systematic approach at an early stage. For those who want to acquire a greater phonic understanding, there are many good books already available. The following books are particularly recommended:

*Beginning to Read* by Marilyn Jager Adams
Published by MIT Press
ISBN 0 262 01112 3

*The Morris-Montessori Word List*
(useful for the early stages as well)
Published by London Montessori Centre Ltd
ISBN 0 948496 80 0

*Alpha to Omega* by Bevé Hornsby and Frula Shear
Published by Heinemann Educational
ISBN 0 435 10382 2

# 6 Parental Involvement

All children want to learn to read when they first start school, and most parents are willing to help them achieve this. The amount of help parents give largely depends on what is asked of them, the child's desire to do the work and the amount of time available. Unfortunately, there are some parents who do not want to be involved in their child's education. These children have to be taught in school only, with extra help from teachers, assistants or other children.

At the beginning of the school year, it is a good idea to invite the parents to a meeting to explain how their children will be taught to read and write. Most parents are interested in learning about the techniques of teaching reading. A parent meeting can take about an hour to cover the various aspects of teaching reading, writing and spelling and to answer questions from the parents.

The meeting might include:

## Sound Sheets with Actions

The parents should know that their children are going to learn the letters that go with the more than 40 sounds in English and to learn to sound out words before being asked to read books by themselves. After parents understand the program their children will participate in, and how they can help, they are usually willing to support the program by helping their child at home.

In most schools, it is unusual to have children who know the letter sounds, and can read and write independently before they start school. If children can read fluently, assure the parents that the children will be given reading books, and would be given help with spelling and learning to write.

Most parents are not aware of the more than 40 sounds, or the fact that they themselves usually figure out unknown words by blending sounds. To demonstrate this, write the following names on a card .... Stoublefund and .... Bloindy. Show the words to the parents and tell them that these are fictional cities, yet you know they can read them. Encourage them to analyze the process they go through. They soon realize that they look at groups of letters, silently pronounce sounds that usually go with those letters and put it all together.

The parents can be given a copy of the list of all the letter sounds from Reproducible Section 12 (page 216). The consonant letters and consonant diagraphs, such as 'sh', 'ch', and 'th' are obvious to parents. However, they are likely to need reminding about different ways in which the vowels are written. These are also listed in Reproducible Section 12 and can be copied for the parents. They will need to know that the children are taught one way of writing the vowels, and then are shown the additional ways. For example, the long 'a' is written as 'ai' at first, as in words like rain, train and pail. Once the majority of children know that, they are taught the other main letters that represent the long 'a' . . . . 'a-e' (late) and '-ay' (day).

The parents can be shown samples of the Sound Sheets, and how the left-hand side of each Sound Sheet has information for parents – including a picture with instructions for the action and a list of words relating to the sound. The Sound Sheets could be reproduced ahead of time and the Parent Information sections cut off and given to the parents at this meeting. Then, as their children are taught the letter sounds, the parents will have the necessary information to help their children at home.

## Sound Books

Parents should know that their children need to be fluent at saying the sounds that go with the letters, and that the Sound Book (see page 133) is for this purpose. Show the parents a sample of a Sound Book and ask them to use the book with their children regularly and make sure the book returns to school every day. They will be able to see how well their child is doing as they use the book with their child.

## Letter Games

Children enjoy learning letter sounds and blending techniques by playing games. There are several games in this handbook with instructions for play in Reproducible Section 11 (pages 203-212):

Pairs Games
Lotto
Reading Games

Demonstrate for the parents how to play the Pairs Games using Sound Book Sheets (Reproducible Section 3, pages 133-140). Parents can also use the cards by saying regular three- or four-letter words such as 'rat', 'bed', 'hop' and 'leg' and asking their child to find the letters and put them in the correct order.

## Word Boxes

Parents should be told the blending technique that helps fluent reading. If the children say the first sound loudly and whisper the rest quickly, they are much more likely to hear the word. To practice this, the children are given words in boxes. Show a sample box and ask the parents to listen to their children blending the letters to read the words. The Word Boxes have words that demonstrate the different ways of writing vowel sounds. Parents can encourage their children to sound the words using the short vowel sound first and if that does not work, then try the long vowel. When the children have mastered the words, they are ready to start reading their own books.

## Reading Books

It is important that children read a little every day at home and at school. Tell parents how to record the pages their child has read at home by crossing out the page numbers on the Reading Card that you send with the book. While their child reads, parents should ask them to sound out the unknown words by themselves and to use context clues. To make sure the child has understood what they have read, parents should talk about the story with their child.

## Independent Writing

Parents need to know that their children will be taught to listen for sounds in words and to write the letters that they think make those sounds. Before this can happen, the children have to know how to write the letters. This is taught when the children are introduced to the Sound Sheets. Parents can help their children learn to write by saying the letters and watching them write the letters. Gentle correction is needed where letters are wrongly formed.

## Homework Writing Books

When the children can write letters and identify the sounds in simple words, they will bring home their Homework Writing Book. Show the parents a sample of the book and a set of the three-letter words from the Homework Writing Sheets in Reproducible Section 5 (pages 155-165). Ask them to say each word from the list for their child. The child has to listen for the sounds and then write the letters for those sounds. Most children manage to do a set of words every day.

## Spelling

In second grade, most children can write sentences by themselves, and will be given a list of spelling words to learn each week. Parents can help by saying the words for their children to write. They should encourage their children to practice the words that they get wrong using the 'LOOK, COVER, WRITE and CHECK' method. Take time at this point to explain this technique to parents.

It is important that parents know about the way their children will be taught to read and write: their support and understanding at home is invaluable to their children's progress.

## *Some Key Points:*

1. Parents are usually very willing to help their children when they know how the children are being taught and what needs to be done.

2. Parents need to be aware that help from them in the beginning teaching of reading and writing will make it easier for their children to master these two vital skills.

3. Parents should be encouraged to:
   a. Use the Sound Books with their children to help them learn the letter sounds.
   b. Play Letter Games helping the children say the letters fluently.
   c. Listen to the children sounding out the words in the Word Boxes.
   d. Dictate the words in the Homework Writing Sheets.
   e. Listen to the children read their books.
   f. Help the children with their weekly spelling homework.

# 7 Summary

This approach to teaching reading, writing and spelling is based on the learner hearing all the sounds of English, not just the sounds of the letters of the alphabet. Each sound is related to a letter or letters, for example, 'm', 'ch' and 'ai'. This is a way of thinking which many people may not be familiar with. As a result, *The Phonics Handbook* presents the teaching methods in some detail, although you may want to adapt these methods to your own style of teaching and the needs of your students. For example, you may prefer your own way of teaching the letter sounds. As long as the sounds are learned in the beginning, it does not matter; the principles are the important factor in this teaching.

The amount of time the teaching takes has been given as a guide. Naturally, some adjustments will have to be made if the majority of the children are slower or faster at learning.

In the beginning, it is recommended that you follow the instructions as closely as possible. In this way, you will know how effective the program is and why it works so well. The children quickly learn the letter sounds when the instruction is concentrated in the first eight weeks. The auditory training will then enable them to take maximum advantage of their letter knowledge.

# PART 2

*Reproducible Section 1*

# Sound Sheets

There are more than 40 sounds in English. In this handbook, 42 of the sounds are taught and the letters that relate to those sounds. By concentrating on teaching the letter sounds before asking children to read books by themselves, most children can learn the sounds in a short period of time. The letters are introduced in an interesting way, involving plenty of actions and fun. Parents contribute by playing letter/word games with their children and regularly going through the children's own Sound Book.

For each of the letter sounds, there is a suggested storyline, an action and a worksheet. Some of the storylines are, of necessity, rather contrived, but they still help the children recognize the sounds. The worksheet has a picture relating to the story for the children to color and a line for them to practice writing. On the left hand side of the sheet, there is information about the action, as well as samples of words using the sound being taught. The suggested storyline has been deliberately kept in note form to help you to tell the story rather than read it.

When the worksheet has been completed, the children take it home to show to their parents. This way parents see the progress being made and are able to join in with the actions.

The Sound Sheets are listed in their recommended order for teaching:

1. s, a, t, i, p, n
2. c k, e, h, r, m, d
3. g, o, u, l, f, b
4. ai, j, oa, ie, ee, or
5. z, w, ng, v, short oo, long oo
6. y, x, ch, sh, voiced th, unvoiced th
7. qu, ou, oi, ue, er, ar

## Suggested Storyline for the 's' sound.

Take a dog for a walk in the country – the dog barks – hears the *sssssssss* sound – see a snake slithering away.

Teacher shows the letter 's'. (Flash Card)

Children weave their arms like a snake while making the *sssssssssssss* sound.

# S s

**ACTION**
Weave like a snake, making s shapes, saying *sssss*.

**snake**
spotty
sun
sit
sand

*Draw the letters dotted here:*

s ss sss

41

## Suggested Storyline for the short 'a' sound.

Pack a picnic basket – children suggest food to be taken – they sit down – spread out the lunch – start eating – a child feels tickling on arm and says *a a a a a a ants* – children jump up and leave the ants.

Teacher shows the letter 'a'. (Flash Card)

Children pretend the ants are going up their arms and say *a a a a.*

# A a

*short a*

**ACTION**
Wiggle fingers above elbow as if ants crawling on you, and say *a, a!*

**ants**

cap
apple
jam
hat

*Draw the letters dotted here:*

43

## Suggested Storyline for the 't' sound.

Children go to a tennis match between two famous people – have great fun watching the match – they watch the people opposite them turning their heads from side to side – children join in turning head every time they hear the 't' sound of the racket hitting the ball.

Teacher shows the letter 't'. (Flash Card)

Children imitate watching tennis turning head from side to side and saying *t t t t*.

# T t

**ACTION**

Children imitate watching tennis, turning head from side to side and saying *t t t t*.

**tennis**

teddy

top

hit

cat

*Draw the letters dotted here:*

45

## Suggested Storyline for the 'i' sound.

Family gets new pet white mouse – argue over what name to give it – leave mouse overnight – mouse gets out of cage – explores room – finds desk – knocks over ink bottle – ink splashes over desk and on to the mouse – children find a very inky mouse in the morning – after that the pet mouse is named 'Inky'.

Teacher shows the letter 'i'. (Flash Card)

Children pretend to be Inky Mouse and wiggle their fingers on the end of their nose saying *i i i i i i*.

### Further Phonics

When children have a better knowledge of the sounds, they can be told that words do not like to end in 'i', so 'y' takes its place in words such as sunny, daddy, silly, happy, etc.

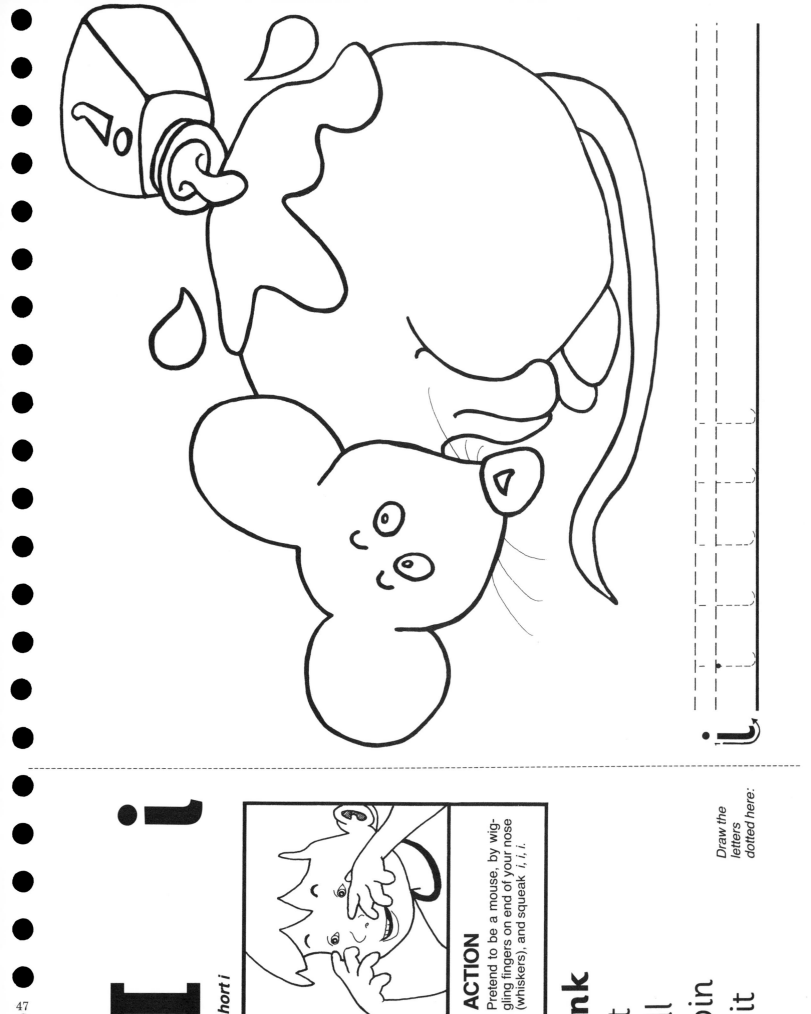

# I i

*short i*

**ACTION**
Pretend to be a mouse, by wiggling fingers on end of your nose (whiskers), and squeak *i, i, i.*

**ink**

it
ill
pin
sit

*Draw the letters dotted here:*

i i

47

## Suggested Storyline for the 'p' sound.

It is a child's birthday − favorite animal is a pig − mother has made a cake in the shape of a pig and has put on the cake five trick candles that relight when blown out − child puffs the candles out, making a *p* sound, but every time the candles appear to have gone out, they light up again.

Teacher shows the letter 'p'. (Flash Card)

Children imagine their finger is a candle and try to puff the trick candle out saying *p p p p p p*.

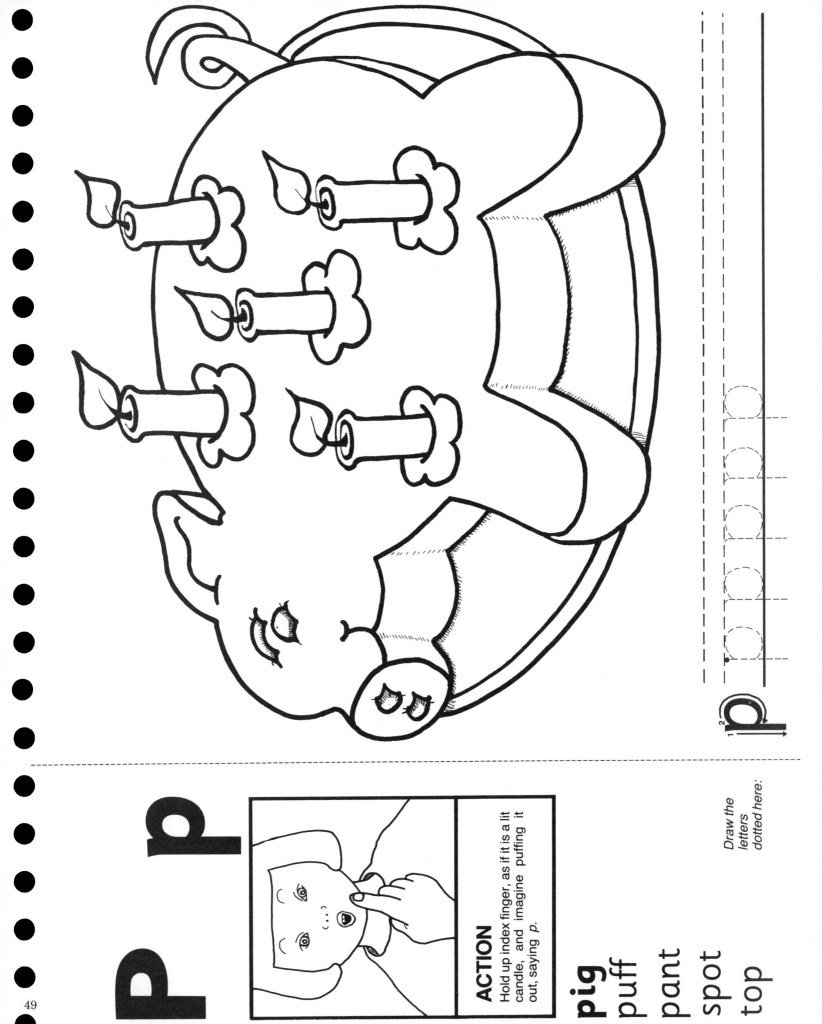

49

# P p

**ACTION**

Hold up index finger, as if it is a lit candle, and imagine puffing it out, saying *p*.

**pig**
puff
pant
spot
top

*Draw the letters dotted here:*

## Suggested Storyline for the 'n' sound.

Child gets a present of a model airplane – goes out to fly it – there is a lot of noise as it takes off – it goes round and round making a *nnnnnnnnn* sound – but then it goes out of control and the airplane nosedives towards the ground, making a louder *nnnnnnnnnnnnnnnn* sound – at the last moment, the airplane pulls out of the nosedive and lands safely.

Teacher shows the letter 'n'. (Flash Card)

Children put their arms out and pretend to be the airplane making a continuous *nnnnnnnnnnn* sound.

# N n

**ACTION**

Hold out arms as if an airplane nose diving, and say *nnnnnnnn.*

**noise**
nosedive
nest
snap
man

*Draw the letters dotted here:*

in nnnnn

## Suggested Storyline for the 'c' and 'k' sound.

Go on vacation to Spain — get in airplane (show 'n' letter again and make *nnnn* noise) — lovely and hot in Spain — spend day on beach — back for dinner — after dinner Spanish dancers perform in hotel — ladies in bright colored dresses with castanets making a *c c c c c* sound.

Teacher shows the letter 'c'. (Flash Card with the 'k' and 'ck' on back)

Children pretend to be a Spanish dancer and click fingers above head saying *c c c c c c*.

### Further Phonics

Children should be told that the 'c' and 'k' both make the same sound and that sometimes they go together in a word. Later, it can be pointed out to the children that 'ck' usually go together at the end of small words with a short vowel.

They also need to know that when 'e', 'i' or 'y' come after a 'c' the sound usually changes to an 's' sound, as in ice, circus, cycle, etc.

### Letter Shapes

The letter k is shown in *The Phonics Handbook* with the familiar open k shape.   Later on the children can learn to write it with the closed k shape.  The closed k shape lets the child write the letter in one movement without taking the pencil off the paper.  Hence it is more suitable for cursive writing.  This closed k shape is used in the other material in *Jolly Phonics*.

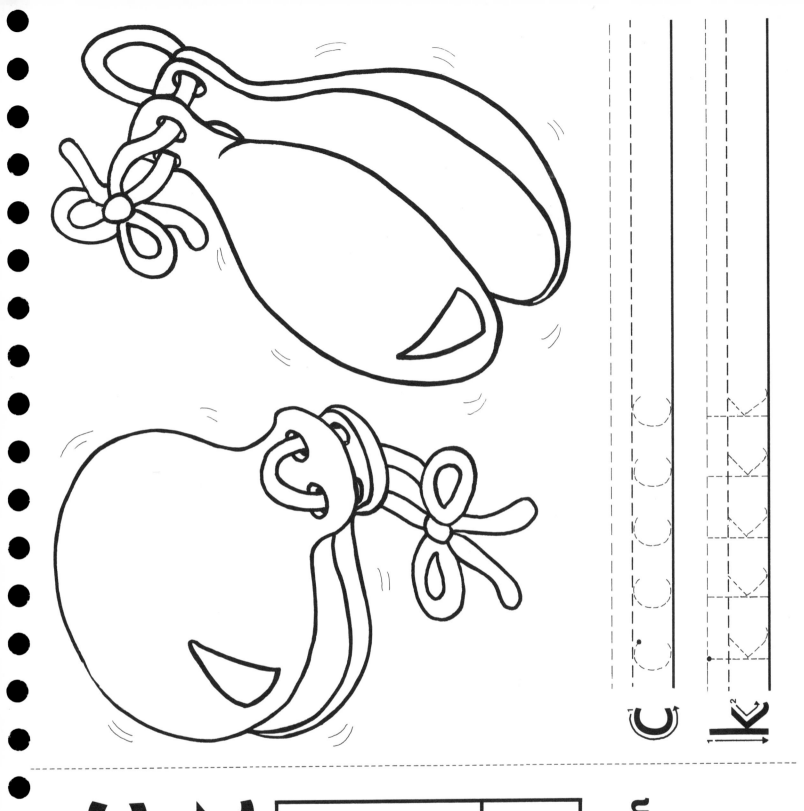

C c

K k

**ACTION**
Raise hands and snap fingers together as if playing castanets, and say *k, k, k.*

**castanets**

**cat** **kitten**

clog king

tractor kite

clock skip

53

## Suggested Storyline for the short 'e' sound.

Children go to stay on farm – lots of different animals – watch the cows being milked – special job given to them – collecting eggs – eggs used for breakfast – everybody comes in to eat eggs – children allowed to fry their own egg for breakfast – crack it open on side of pan saying *e e e e e egg*.

Teacher shows the letter 'e'. (Flash Card)

Children pretend to hold egg in one hand and tap it against the pan saying *e e e*, then use both hands to open egg shell and say *e*.

# E e

*short e*

**ACTION**

Pretend to hold egg with one hand, as if cracking it against the side of a bowl or pan. Use both hands to open shell, saying *eh eh eh.*

**egg**
empty
end
shed
tent

*Draw the letters dotted here:*

55

## Suggested Storyline for the 'h' sound.

School has a sports day – some children in the hopping race – by the time they get to the end they are panting and saying *h h h h h*.

Teacher shows the letter 'h'. (Flash Card)

Children pretend they are panting, and say *h h h h h h*.

# H h

**ACTION**

Act as if panting after a race, holding hand up to mouth, and saying *h, h, h.*

**h**op
hot
huff
house
hill

*Draw the letters dotted here:*

h

## Suggested Storyline for the 'r' sound.

The family has a puppy – very playful – it has a favorite piece of ragged blanket in its bed – mother wants to wash the blanket and tries to take it away – puppy holds on to the blanket with its mouth and shakes its head making a *rrrrrrrrrrrrr* sound.

Teacher shows the letter 'r'. (Flash Card)

Children pretend to be the puppy holding the blanket, shaking their heads and making a *rrrrrrrrrrrrr* sound.

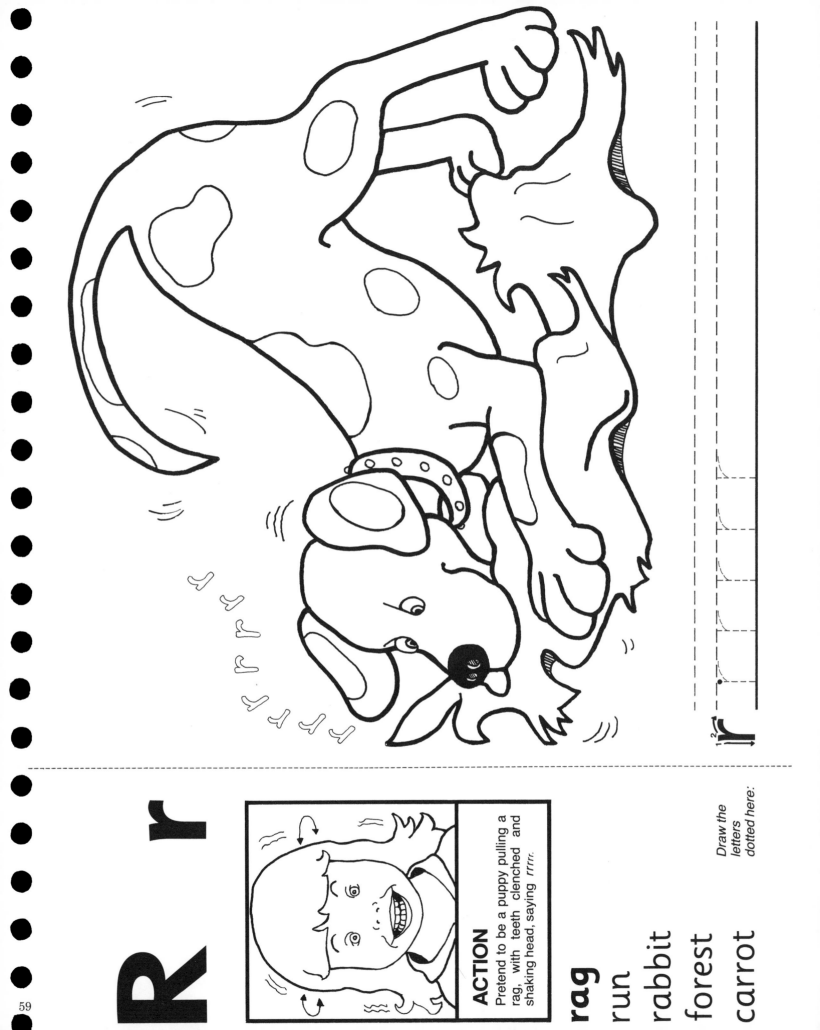

# R  r

**ACTION**

Pretend to be a puppy pulling a rag, with teeth clenched and shaking head, saying *rrrr*.

rag
run
rabbit
forest
carrot

*Draw the letters dotted here:*

## Suggested Storyline for the 'm' sound.

Children allowed to choose their favorite meal – each time a child describes a favorite meal, everybody rubs tummy and says *mmmmmmmmmmmmmm.*

Teacher shows the letter 'm'. (Flash Card)

Children rub tummy and say *mmmmmmmmmmmmmmm.*

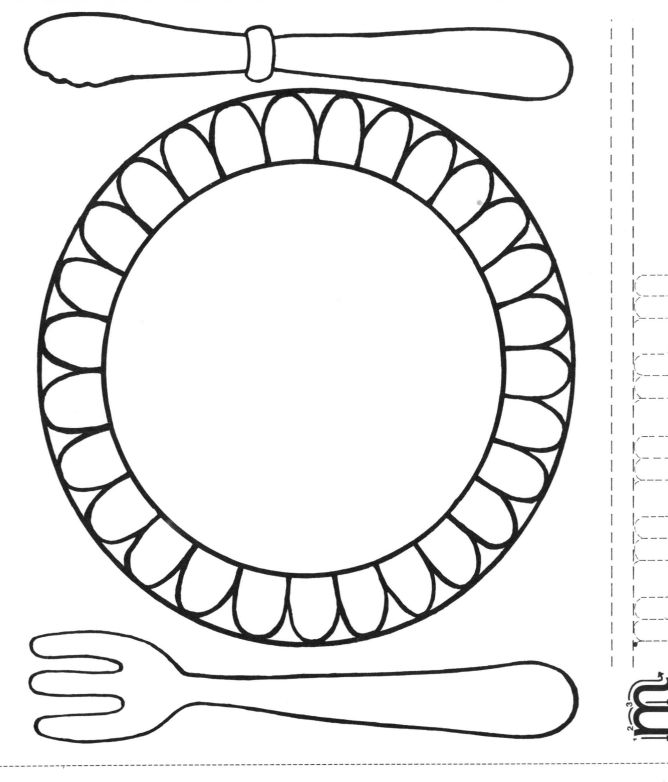

# Mm

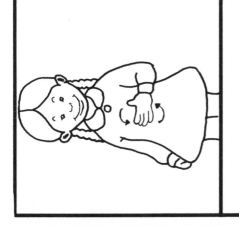

**ACTION**
Rub tummy, seeing tasty food, and say *mmmm*.

**meal**
menu
man
summer
swim

*Draw the letters dotted here:*

61

## Suggested Storyline for the 'd' sound.

Child helps older brother to clear out his old toys – at the back finds drum – child starts playing it, making a *d d d d d* sound.

Teacher shows the letter 'd'. (Flash Card)

Children pretend to be playing a drum, moving hands up and down saying *d d d d d*.

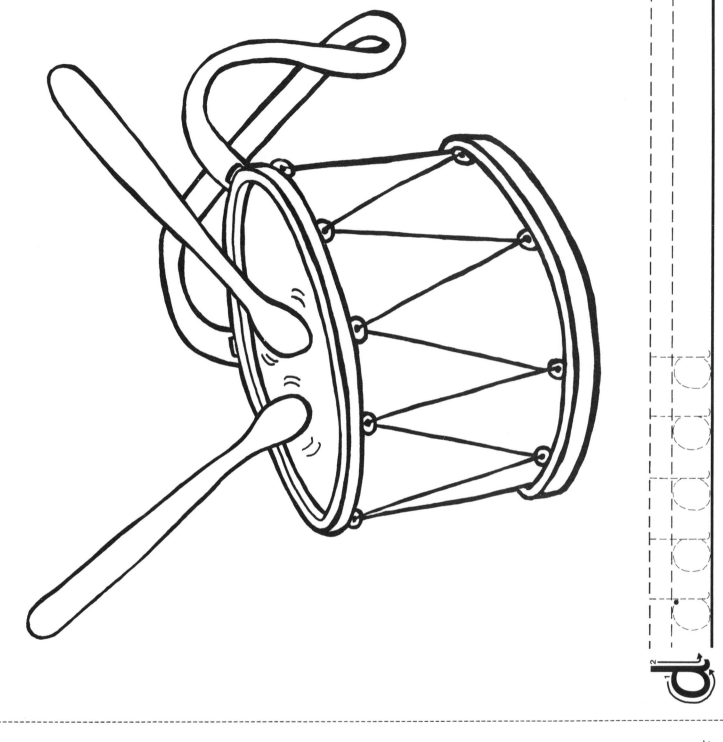

# D d

**ACTION**
Pretend to hold drum sticks and beat up and down on a drum and say *d d d d*.

**drum**
band
dog
sad
puddle

*Draw the letters dotted here:*

d

## Suggested Storyline for the 'g' sound.

A sink is clogged and full of water – call for the plumber – the sink is unclogged and as the water goes down the drain, it makes a gurgling sound *g g g g g g*.

Teacher shows the letter 'g'. (Flash Card)
Children pretend their hand is the water going round and round down the drain saying *g g g g g g g*.

### Further Phonics

When an 'e', 'i' or 'y' comes after a 'g' the sound usually changes to a 'j' as in gentle, giraffe, gymnast, etc.

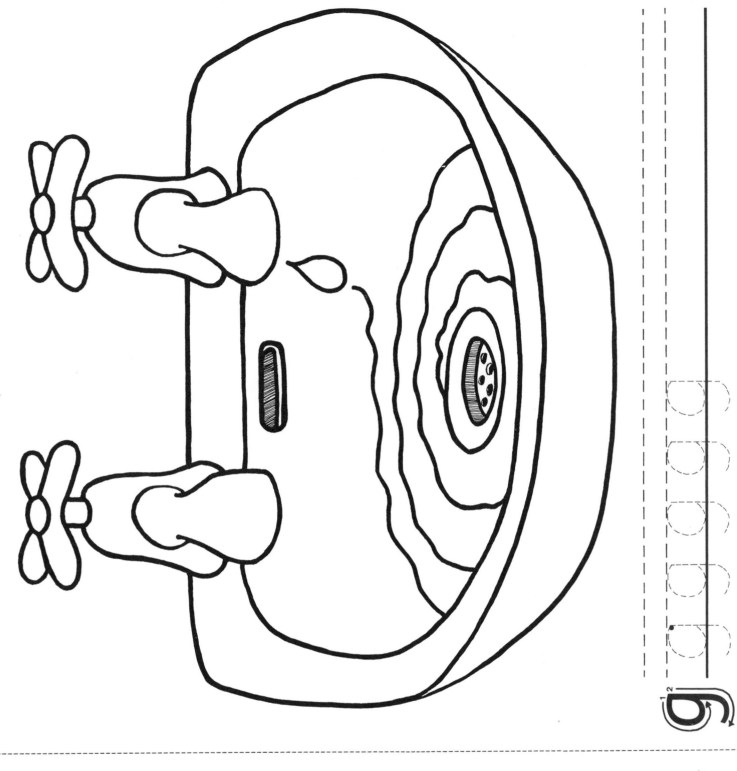

# G g

**ACTION**

Children pretend their hand is the water going round and round down the drain saying *g, g, g, gurgle.*

**g**lug
gurgle
goose
girl
leg

*Draw the letters dotted here:*

g²

g

## Suggested Storyline for the short 'o' sound.

Family moves into a new house – child has a new bedroom – can reach the light switch from bed – plays turning light on and off saying *o o, o o, o o, on off* – until daddy stops him.

Teacher shows the letter 'o'. (Flash Card)

Children point finger, as if pushing switch on and off saying *o o, o o, o o, o o.*

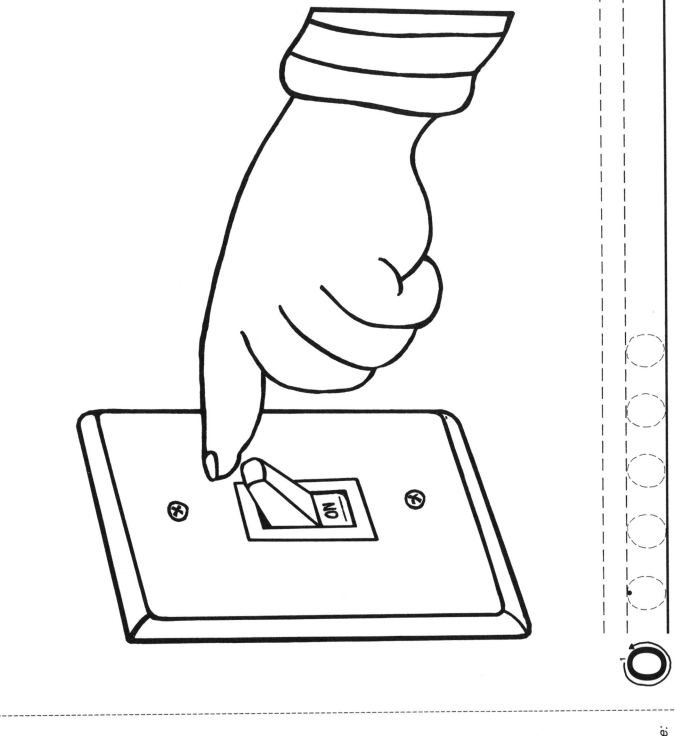

*short o*

**ACTION**
Imagine turning switch on and off, and say *o, o; o, o; on, off.*

**on off**
octopus
ostrich
pond
shop

*Draw the letters dotted here:*

67

## Suggested Storyline for the short 'u' sound.

Family goes out for a walk on a very sunny day – one child insists on taking new umbrella – everybody laughs at child – BUT during the day it does begin to rain – up goes the umbrella – child says *u up ... u up .... umbrella* – child keeps dry – everybody else gets wet!

Teacher shows the letter 'u'. (Flash Card)

Children make upward motion with hand, as if putting up an umbrella saying *u u u u u u.*

# U u

*short u*

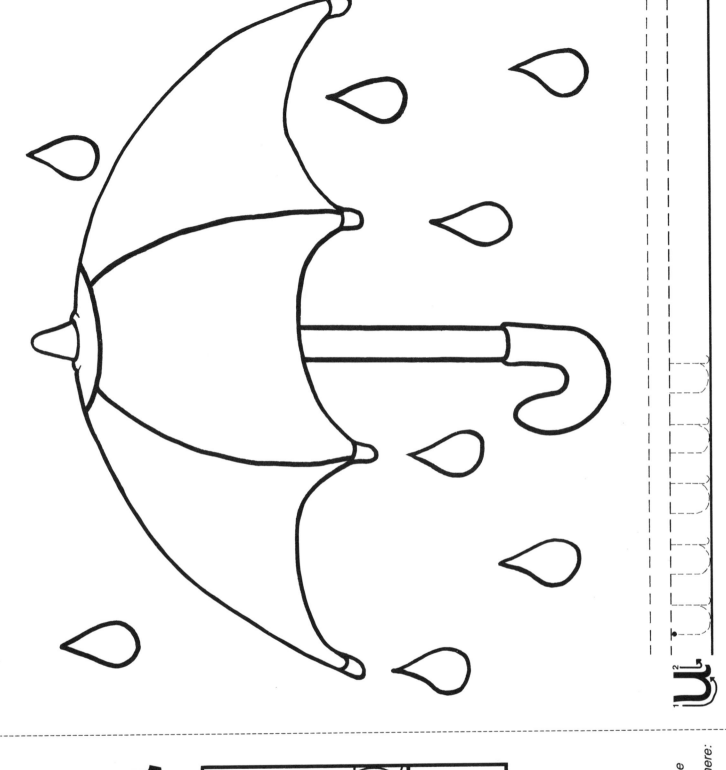

**ACTION**
Keep one hand steady and raise the other, as if raising an umbrella, and say *u...u...u...up.*

**up**
umbrella
under
sun
jump

*Draw the letters dotted here:*

## Suggested Storyline for the 'l' sound.

Child's birthday party — mother puts a fancy lollipop at each child's place — after cake and ice cream, the children unwrap the lollipops — they lick the lollipops saying *l l l l l l l lick, l l l l l l l lick, l l l l l l l lollipop.*

Teacher shows the letter 'l'. (Flash Card)

Children put out their tongues, pretending to be licking a lollipop saying *l l l l l l l l.*

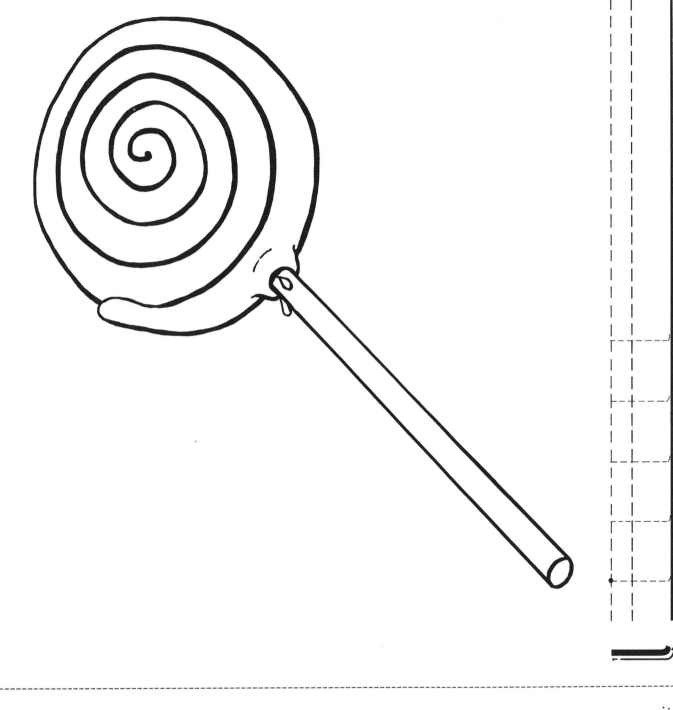

# Ll

**ACTION**
Pretend to lick a lollipop, saying
*lllll.*

**lollipop**
lick
lemon
spell
sleep

*Draw the letters dotted here:*

## Suggested Storyline for the 'f' sound.

Children are given a big inflatable fish that can be used in the water — they take it to the beach — father holds the rope attached to the fish — children play on it — they hear a *fffffffff* sound — fish begins to deflate.

Teacher shows the letter 'f'. (Flash Card)

Children bring their hands together as if the fish is deflating, making a *fffffffff* sound.

**Letter Shapes**

The letter f is shown in *The Phonics Handbook* with the familiar f shape that is all 'above the line'. Later on the the children can learn to write it with a descender so it looks more like ∫. With a descender the letter is easier to write in cursive writing (and is less likely to be confused with a t). This ∫ with a descender is used in the other material in *Jolly Phonics*.

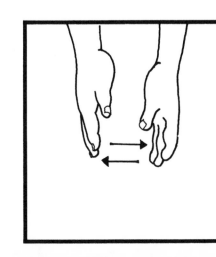

# F f

**ACTION**
Place one hand above the other, lower the top hand as if inflatable fish is deflating, and say *fffffffff.*

**fish**

flat

fun

soft

stiff

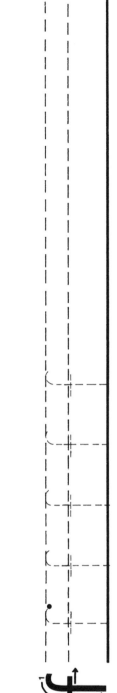

*Draw the letters dotted here:*

## Suggested Storyline for the 'b' sound.

Children go to the park – play baseball – as the bat hits the ball it makes a *b* sound.

Teacher shows the letter 'b'. (Flash Card)

Children pretend to hold a bat and hit a ball saying *b b b b b b b b b*. Show them the correct formation of the letter by thinking of the downstroke of the *b* as the bat and the round part of the *b* as the ball. They hit the ball along the line, with the bat, when writing.

# B b

**ACTION**

Place hands together as if holding a bat and hitting a baseball, saying *b, b, b*.

**bat**
baseball
belt
tubby
crab

*Draw the letters dotted here:*

## Suggested Storyline for the 'ai' sound.

A child was having difficulty hearing – every time spoken to put hand over ear and said *ai* – mother got very annoyed – took him to the doctor – doctor found wax in ears – cleaned them – no more *ai*'s!

Teacher shows the letters 'ai'. (Flash Card)

Children pretend to be child and put hand over ear and say *ai*.

### Further Phonics

The long 'a' vowel has got two other main ways of being written:

a-e ... as in cake, late, fame, same, shape, etc.

ay ... as in day, play, stay, way, etc. This is really the 'ai' but because it usually comes at the end, the 'i' changes to a 'y'.

# ai

*long a*

**ACTION**
Cup hand over ear, as if hard of hearing, and say ay?

**aim**
snail
rain
pain
train

*Draw the letters dotted here:*

77

## Suggested Storyline for the 'j' sound.

A friend is coming to play – children in family ask for Jello – mother makes Jello – when it is ready she tips it on to a plate – Jello wobbles – children wobble like the Jello saying *j j j j j jello.*

Teacher shows the letter 'j'. (Flash Card)

Children pretend to be the Jello. They wrap arms round their body saying *j j j j j j j j j.*

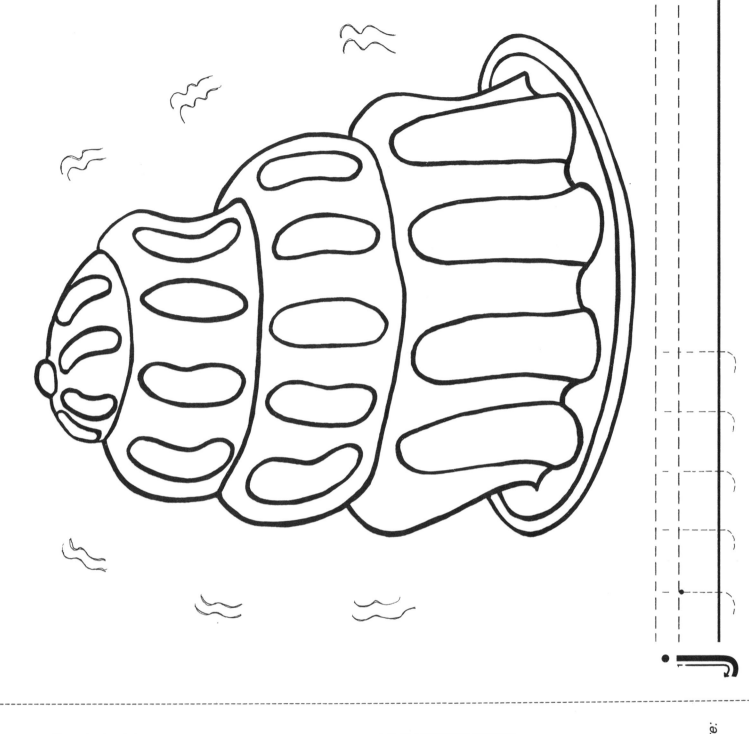

# j J

### ACTION
Pretend to be a Jello, and
wobble, saying *j, j, j, jello.*

## Jello
jump
jet
jug
jam

*Draw the
letters
dotted here:*

j J

## Suggested Storyline for the 'oa' sound.

It is a windy day — family go to feed goats in a field — see oak tree has fallen down trapping a goat in the branches — so shocked, they say *oa, oa* poor goat — they free the goat.

Teacher shows the letters 'oa'. (Flash Card)

Children pretend to see the oak tree. They put their hand over their mouth and say *oa, oa*.

### Further Phonics

The long 'o' vowel has got three other main ways of being written:

o-e  .... bone, stone, home, phone, etc.

oe  .... toe, hoe, doe, foe, etc.

ow  .... pillow, follow, snow, slow, marrow, etc.

## oa

*long o*

**ACTION**

Bring hand up to mouth as if see-ing something go wrong, and say *oh!*

**oak**

goat

coat

soak

toast

*Draw the letters dotted here:*

oa

## Suggested Storyline for the 'ie' sound.

A child goes to a fancy dress party in a sailor suit – a friend shows the child how to stand to attention and salute saying: *"ie ie"*.

Teacher shows the letters 'ie'. (Flash Card)

Children pretend to be the sailor and salute saying: *ie ie*.

### Further Phonics

The long 'ie' vowel has got three other main ways of being written:

i-e  .... like, bike, size, wipe, etc.
y    .... my, try, fry, cycle, etc.
igh  .... right, night, bright, sight, etc.

.ie

long i

**tie**
pie
die
lie

**ACTION**
Stand to attention and salute, saying *aye aye*.

Draw the letters
dotted here:

.ie .ie .ie .ie

ie₁ ie₂

83

## Suggested Storyline for the sounds 'ee' and 'or'.

A donkey is retired from giving children rides on the beach — goes to live in a field — some children go to see the donkey everyday — they take carrots for the donkey — when the donkey sees them, it greets them by waggling it's ears and braying — except it doesn't make the normal 'hee haw' sound, it says *'ee or'* — so the children call him Eeyore.

Teacher shows the letters 'ee' and 'or'. (Flash Cards). Ensure that the children recognise these as separate sounds. Hold the correct Flash Card up as each sound is spoken.

Children pretend their hands are the donkey's ears, by putting them on top of their head. Their hands are straight up for the *ee* and bent down for the *or* when saying *ee or, ee or*.

**Further Phonics.**

The long 'ee' vowel has got one other main way of being written:

ea  .... peas, dream, cream, stream, etc.

The 'or' sound has three other main ways of being written. These other ways do not have an 'r' in the spelling, and are sounded without the 'r' sound in 'or':

au  .... August, sauce, fraud, haul, etc.
aw  .... jaw, yawn, shawl, raw, etc.
al  .... talk, walk, chalk, ball, etc.

# ee
# or

*long e and the 'or' sound*

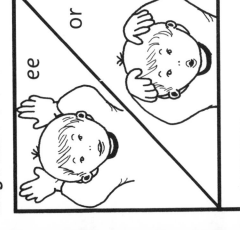

**ACTION**
Pretend to be a donkey braying, and saying *eeyore, eeyore*.

**bee**   **fork**

see   short

sheep   torch

feet   corn

tree   storm

ee

or

## Suggested Storyline for the 'z' sound.

Children watch a bee in the garden – it goes from flower to flower – everytime it flies it makes a *zzzzzzzzzzzzz* sound.

Teacher shows the letter 'z'. (Flash Card)

Children pretend to be bees by keeping their elbows in and flapping their arms up and down saying *zzzzzzzzzzzzzzzzzz*.

# Z z

**ACTION**
Pretend to be a bee, with elbows in, and hands flapping, saying zzzzzzzzzzz.

**zebra**
buzz
zoo
zipper
fizzy

*Draw the letters dotted here:*

## Suggested Storyline for the 'w' sound.

Tell the Aesop Fable of 'The Wind and the Sun' – how the West wind lost the competition to get the man to take his coat off – in the story, everytime the wind blows, the children pretend to be the wind and blow on to their hands saying *wwwwww wind.*

Teacher shows the letter 'w'. (Flash Card)

Children cup hands and blow on to them saying *wwwwww.*

### Further Phonics

The 'w' sound has got another way of being written:

wh . . . . white, whale, whip, wheel, etc. plus the six question words:
. . . . when, where, what, why, who (silent 'w') and which.

# Ww

**ACTION**
Blow onto open hand like the wind, repeating *wh, wh, wh*.

**wind**
wet
west
windmill
swift

*Draw the letters dotted here:*

W

## Suggested Storyline for the 'ng' sound.

Children watch weight lifting on television – they laugh at the strange faces and noises – they then pretend they are weight lifters, using broom and pulling a face, and say *ngngngng*.

Teacher shows the letters 'ng'. (Flash Card)

Children pretend to be lifting weight and say *ngngngng*.

# ng

**ACTION**

Pretend to be a weight lifter, bringing arms above head, and say *ng*....

**strong**
ring
song
string
bang

*Draw the letters dotted here:*

ng ng ng ng ng

## Suggested Storyline for the 'v' sound.

Uncle Vic arrives in a van — asks if child would like to come with him to pick up some people from the station — get to station — find people — drives off dropping people at their houses — each time child pretends to be driving, making *vvvvvvvvvvvvv* sound.

Teacher shows the letter 'v'. (Flash Card)

Children pretend to be driving, holding the steering wheel and saying *vvvvvvvvvvvvv*.

# V v

Vic's van

**ACTION**
Pretend to be driving along in a van, saying *vvvv.*

**van**
vest
velvet
very
drive

*Draw the letters dotted here:*

V

93

## Suggested Storyline for the short 'oo' and long 'oo' sounds.

Children are taken round an old house – see a cuckoo clock on the wall – it is nearly 12 o'clock – they wait to see what happens – as 12 o'clock strikes the cuckoo pops in and out of the clock saying *"oo oo, oo oo"*.

Teacher shows the short 'oo' and long 'oo' letters. (Flash Card)

Children pretend to be the cuckoo poking it's head in and out of the clock saying *oo oo, oo oo*.

### Further Phonics

Initially these two sounds are written slightly differently. The short 'oo', as in foot, has been compressed, so that the children can tell the difference. The children can be told that in books the two 'oo's are the same size. They simply have to try blending both sounds, to see which one gives them the word.

The short 'oo' sound has got another main way of being written:

u     .... cuckoo, put, pull, pudding, etc.

The long 'oo' sound has got three other ways of being written:

u-e   .... rude, June, flute, rule, etc.
ue    .... blue, clue, glue, true, etc.
ew    .... blew, yew, flew, screw, etc.

**Short and long oo**

**ACTION**

Imagine being the cuckoo in a cuckoo clock, jutting head forward and back, saying the call of the cuckoo: *u, oo; u, oo.*

**cook**   **coo**

book      moon

look      soon

hook      shoot

took      tooth

oo

## Suggested Storyline for the 'y' sound.

A child goes shopping with daddy — chooses yellow yogurt to have after dinner — the child eats the yogurt saying *yyyyyyummy, yyyyyyellow, yyyyyyogurt.*

Teacher shows the letter 'y'. (Flash Card)

Children pretend to eat yogurt. With each spoonful they say *y y y y y.*

# Y y

**ACTION**
Pretend to eat yogurt from a spoon, saying y, y, yogurt, with each spoonful.

**yogurt**
yellow
yo-yo
yes
yard

*Draw the letters dotted here:*

97

## Suggested Storyline for the 'x' sound.

Aliens land – they leave their space craft, carrying x-ray guns – they have come to meet the people – some people are frightened and attack the aliens – the aliens point their x-ray guns at them – they are turned into stone for a time – the other people make friends and have a party!

Teacher shows the letter 'x'. (Flash Card)

Children make gun shape with hand and pretend to shoot saying *x x x x x x*.

It should be pointed out that 'x' is really two sounds, a 'k' and a 's'. Ask the children to 'sound out' words with 'x' in, such as: fox, box, six, mix. By putting up a finger for each sound they hear, they will see that there are four sounds in these words.

# X x

**ACTION**
Pretend to take an x-ray with an x-ray gun, saying *ks, ks, ks*.

**x-ray**

fox

six

box

mix

*Draw the letters dotted here:*

99

## Suggested Storyline for the 'ch' sound.

Children go on a steam train – when they return home they play trains in the garden – as they go along they say *ch ch ch ch ch*.

Teacher shows the letters 'ch'. (Flash Card)

Children pretend to be a steam train and move bent arms backwards and forwards saying *ch ch ch ch ch*.

## ch

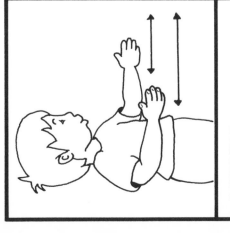

**ACTION**
Pretend to be a steam train, moving the arms like piston rods, and saying *ch...ch...ch.*

**choo-choo**
chick
church
chop
lunch

ch

*Draw the letters dotted here:*

## Suggested Storyline for the 'sh' sound.

Baby keeps crying – goes to sleep at last – sister comes along – mother puts her finger to her lips and says *shshshshshshsh*.

Teacher shows the letters 'sh'. (Flash Card)

Children pretend to be the mother and say *shshshshshshsh*.

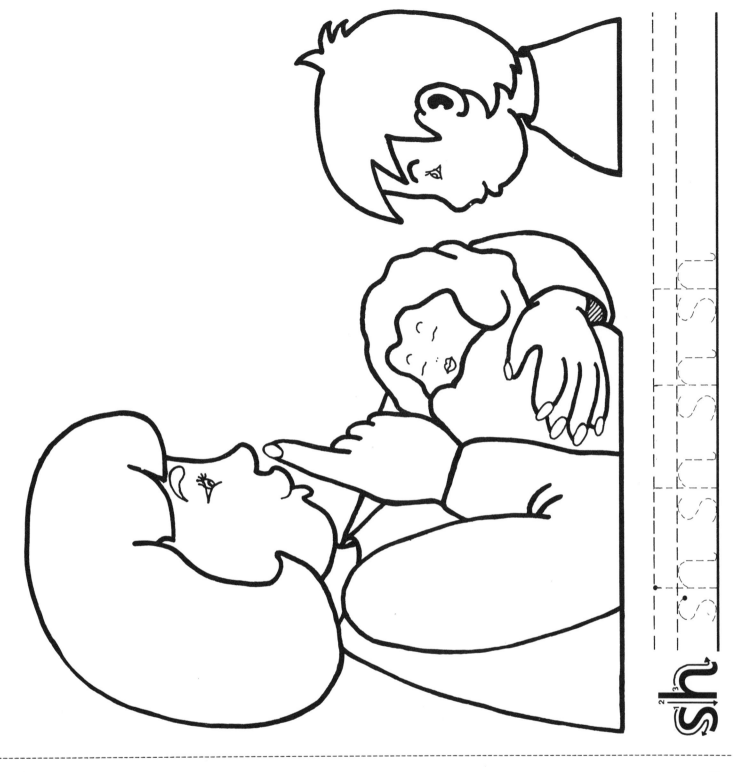

# sh

**ACTION**

Place index finger over lips, and say *sh*.

**ship**
shell
shout
dish
crash

sh

*Draw the letters dotted here:*

## Suggested Storyline for the voiced 'th' and unvoiced 'th' sounds.

Family goes to the circus – the clowns are their favorite – one clown was a little bit rude, and put the tip of his tongue out and made a funny sound *thththththththth* (voiced 'th', as in this) – but another clown was big and very rude – he kept sticking his tongue out a long way, saying *thththththththth* (unvoiced 'th' as in thin).

Teacher shows the letters 'th' and 'th'. (Flash Cards)

Initially, as with the 'oo', the two sounds have been written slightly differently. The shorter, voiced 'th' has been compressed, so that the children can not only hear the difference but see it as well. They can be soon told that in books there is no difference. They simply have to try both sounds to see which one goes with the word.

Children pretend to be the less rude clown by sticking out their tongue a little and saying *thththththththth* (voiced as in 'this') and the very rude clown by sticking their tongue far out saying *thththththththth* (whispered as in 'thin').

# th th

*voiced and unvoiced th*

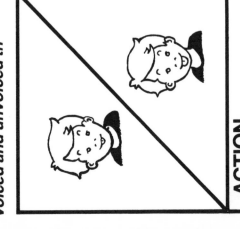

**ACTION**
Child pretends to be a little rude by sticking out tongue a little and saying *th* (as in them), and very rude by sticking tongue further out and saying *th* (as in thumb).

**that** **thin**

then thumb

this thick

feather thunder

with moth

## Suggested Storyline for the 'qu' sound.

Children go to the park to feed the ducks – they pretend to be ducks by saying *qu qu qu qu quack*.

Teacher shows the letters 'qu'. (Flash Card)

There are two letters for 'qu' and two sounds 'k-w'. The children should be aware of this, so that when they hear the sounds 'kw' in a word, they know it is likely to be written as 'qu'.

Children make hands into ducks bill while saying *qu qu qu qu qu*.

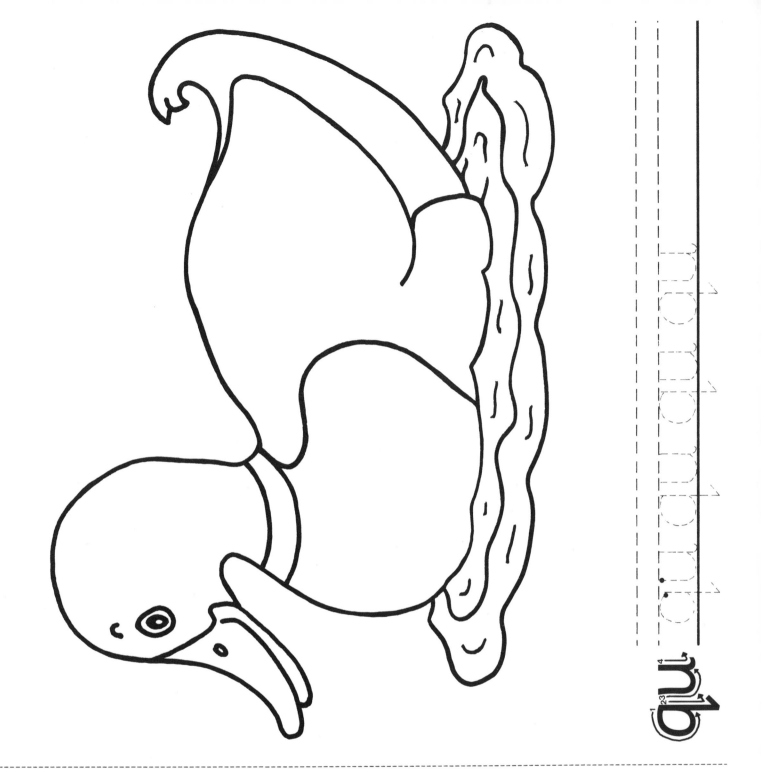

# Qq

# Qu qu

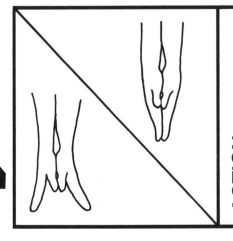

**ACTION**
Make a duck's beak with hinged hands, and say *qu, qu, qu, quack.*

**quack**

queen

quick

quiet

squirrel

*Draw the letters dotted here:*

qu qu qu qu qu qu

qu

## Suggested Storyline for the 'ou' sound.

A child is learning to sew − threads needle − makes a few stitches − brings needle up and accidently pricks thumb and says *ou*.

Teacher shows the letters 'ou'. (Flash Card)

Children pretend their finger is a needle and stabs at thumb on the other hand saying *ou*.

**Further Phonics**

'ou' can be written as:

'ow' .... cow, crown, brown.

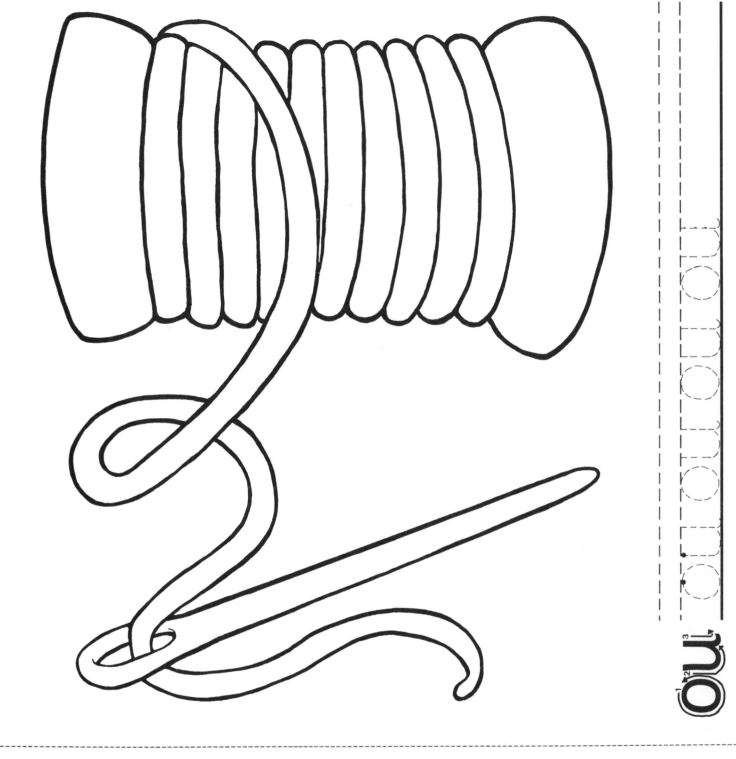

## ou

*the 'ou' sound*

**ACTION**
Pretend your finger is a needle, and prick thumb, saying *ow!*

**ouch!**

out

loud

cloud

sound

Draw the letters dotted here:

ou

## Suggested Storyline for the 'oi' sound.

Sailors are on their ship – ship develops engine trouble and they need help – they look out for another ship – see one at last and shout *oi – ship ahoy*.

Teacher shows the letters 'oi'. (Flash Card)

Children cup hands round mouth, as if hailing the other ship, and say *oi*.

### Further Phonics

'oi' can be written as:

'oy' .... joy, boy, toy, etc. – usually at the end because words do not like to end in 'i' and change to 'y'.

## oi

the 'oi' sound

**ACTION**

Cup hands around mouth as if hailing a passing boat, saying *oi, ship ahoy!*

oil
coin
point
boil
join

*Draw the letters dotted here:*

oi

## Suggested Storyline for the 'ue' sound.

Children at a birthday party – playing games – play a game where the child is in the middle of a circle of children and has to guess who has got the ring – the child has to point and say "I think it is *ue*."

Teacher shows the letters 'ue'. (Flash Card)

Children point finger and say *ue*.

### Further Phonics

The two other main ways of writing 'ue' are:

u-e ....cube, cute, mule, etc.
ew  ....few, skew, ewe, etc.

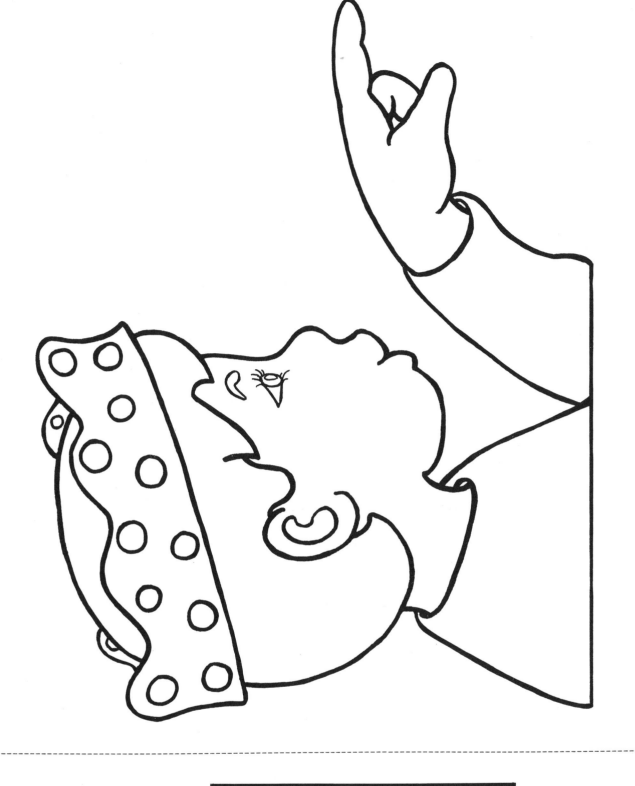

# ue

*long u*

**ACTION**

Point to different people around you, and say *you...you...you*

**argue**

cue

rescue

barbecue

statue

ue ue ue ue ue

*Draw the letters dotted here:*

113

## Suggested Storyline for the 'er' sound.

Children help mom make some gingerbread people – they help put the ingredients into the bowl, mixing each in thoroughly with the mixer making *errrrr errrrrr* sound – afterwards have fun putting faces on the gingerbread people.

Teacher shows the letters 'er'. (Flash Card)

Children pretend to be mixer and roll their hands over and over saying *errrrrrrr*.

### Further Phonics

There are three other main ways of writing the 'er' sound, the last of which does not have the 'r' in the spelling and is sounded without the 'r' sound:

ir    .... girl, bird, shirt, etc.
ur    .... burn, turn, curl, etc.
e     .... tunnel, squirrel, garden, etc.

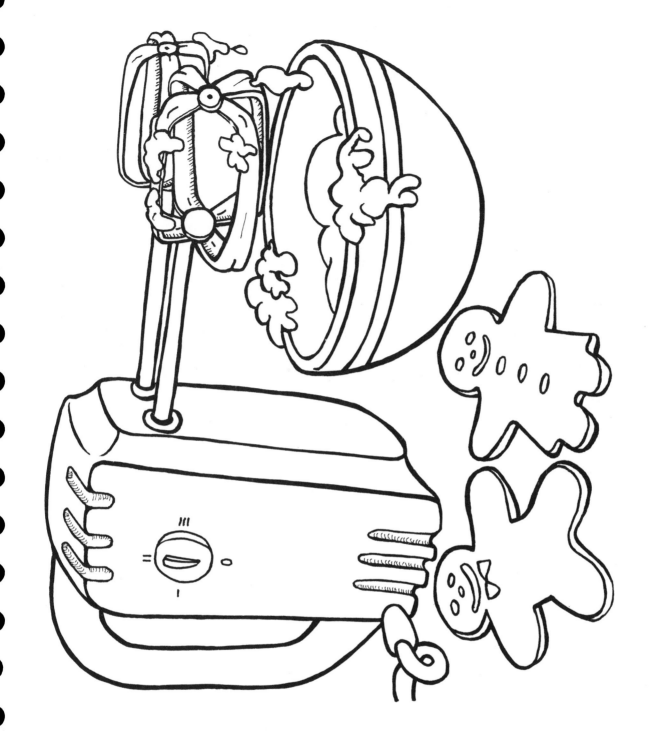

# er

*the 'er' sound*

**ACTION**

Roll hands over and over each other, and say *er, er* (as in *the* or *her*.

**mixer**

term

her

sister

dinner

*Draw the letters dotted here:*

er er er er

## Suggested Storyline for the 'ar' sound.

A child comes home with a sore throat — the next morning it is still very sore — mother makes an appointment with the doctor — doctor looks into the throat and asks the child to say *ahahahahah.*

Teacher shows the letters 'ar'. (Flash Card)
Children pretend their throat is sore and open their mouths and say *ahahahahahah.*

### Further Phonics

The 'ar' sound can be written without the 'r' in the spelling, and in these words it is sounded without the 'r' sound:

a     .... father, ma, palm.

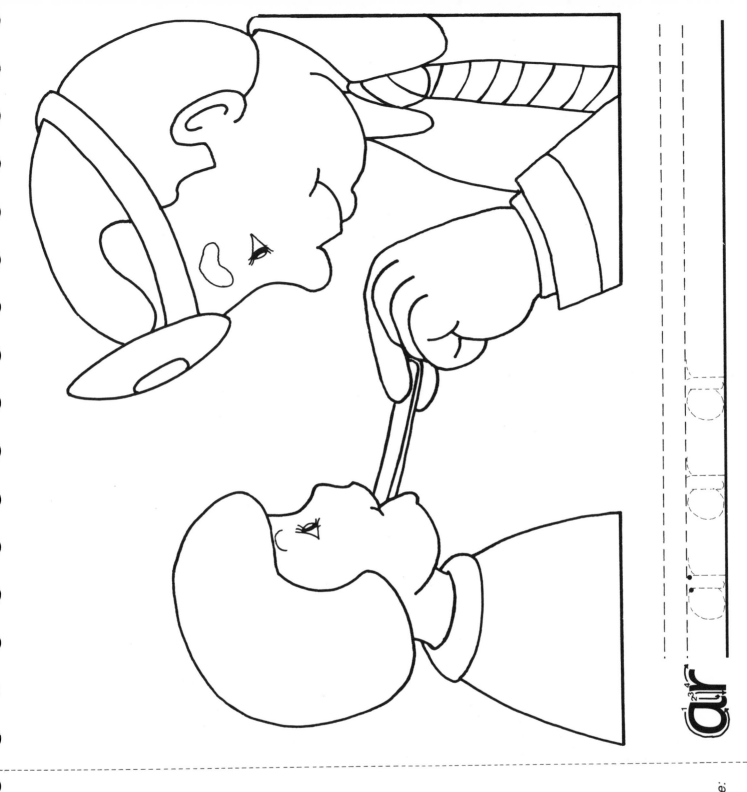

# ar
### the 'ar' sound

**ACTION**
Open mouth wide and say *ah.*

**arm**
car
park
dark
star

*Draw the letters dotted here:*

## Reproducible Section 2

# Flash Card Sheets

Once the children have learned the letter sounds from the Sound Sheets, they will need to become very fluent at recognizing sounds. Flash Cards for each letter sound are very useful in achieving this, and could be used every day. As you hold up the letters the children say the sounds.

You can make Flash Cards for each letter sound from copies of the Flash Card Sheets. As a further help, the back of each sheet has the phonic alternatives, which can be copied to form the back of the Flash Cards. These can be used when the alternatives have been taught, and you want to review them.

The Flash Card Sheets have the letter sounds grouped in the recommended teaching order.

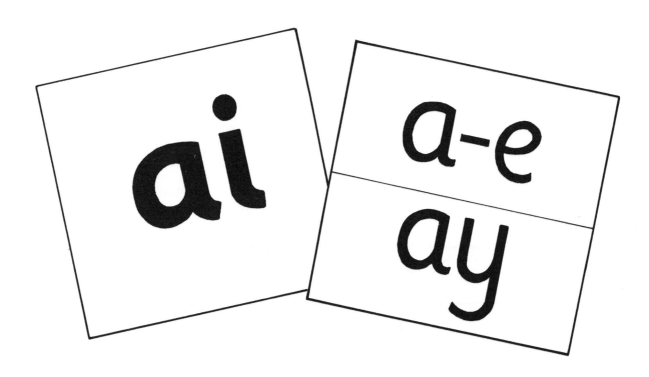

s

a

t

i

p

n

y

c

e

h

r

m

d

k

g

o

u

l

f

b

j

ai

oa

ie

ee

or

a-e

ay

i-e

o-e

igh | y

ow | oe

ore | al

ea

au | aw

z

w

ng

v

oo

oo

wh

nk

u-e

| ue | ew |

y

x

ch

sh

th

th

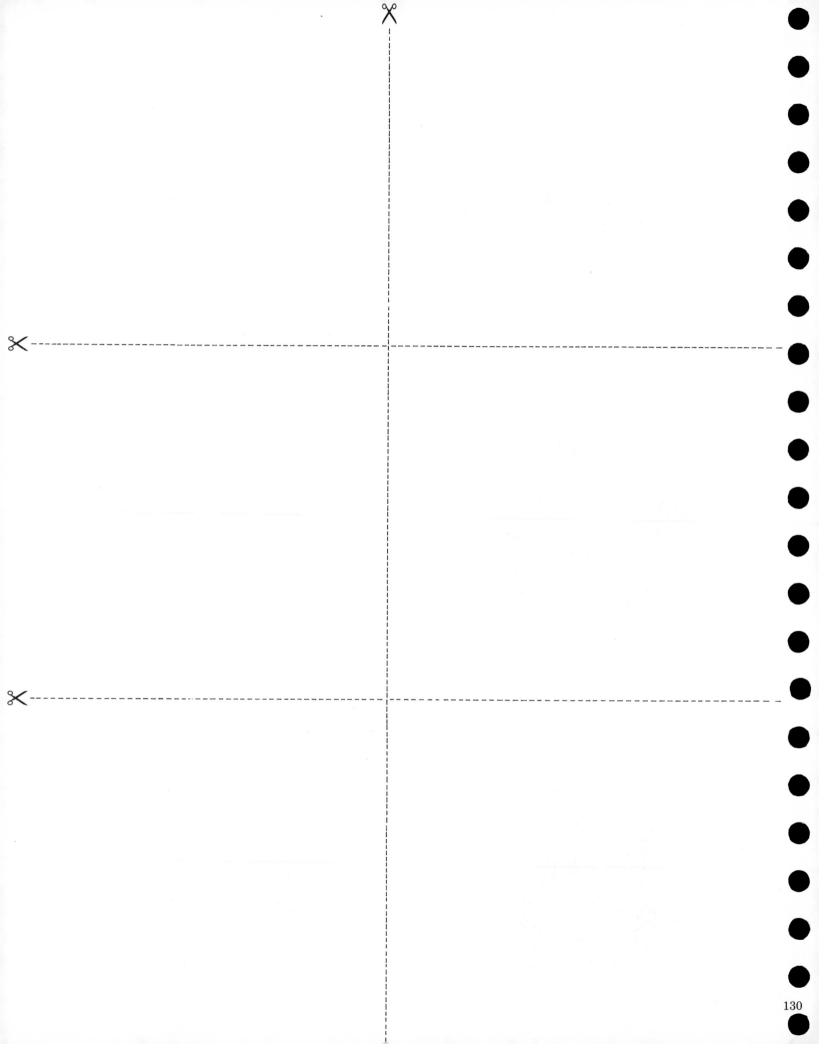

qu

ou

oi

ue

er

ar

ow

u-e

ew

oy

a

ir

ur

*Reproducible Section 3*

# Sound Book Sheets

A Sound Book should be prepared for each child by stapling together sheets of plain paper, cutting in half if necessary so that the book is not too large. As the letter sounds are taught, the letters are glued in the child's Sound Book. The letters have been printed on the following pages in the recommended teaching order, ready to be reproduced, cut up, and glued in the books at the appropriate time. The children take their books home and go through it with their parents. This not only reinforces the letter sounds but also the left to right orientation of books.

The children should bring their Sound Book to school every day. You can then go through the book regularly with each child to see how well they are learning the letter sounds. Visual rewards, such as stars stuck on the cover, provide much encouragement to parents and children alike and stimulate further interest and improvement.

As soon as the first six letters have been taught, the first Sound Book Sheet (the one with s, a, t, etc.) should be reproduced for each child to take home. The letters have been printed twice on each sheet so that parents can glue the extra letters on a piece of card stock, cut them out and play 'Pairs' and other games with their child. The instructions for these games are on page 205 in the Reproducible Section 11.

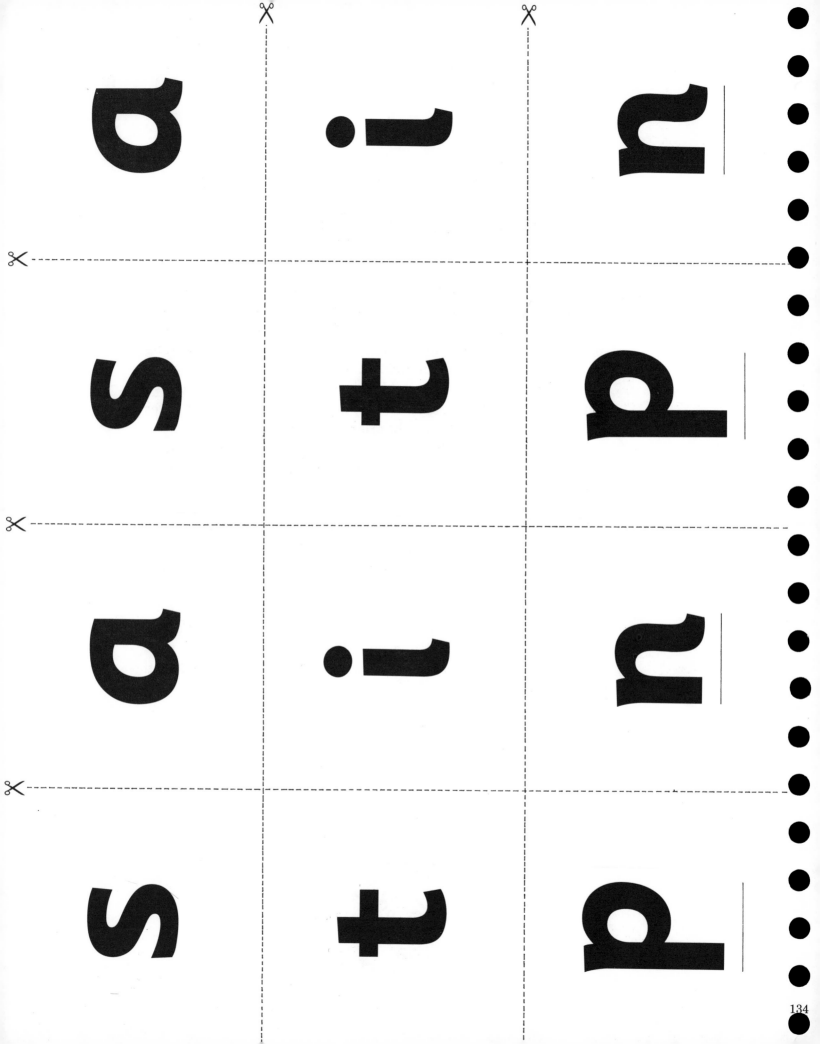

a s i t n p
a s i t n p

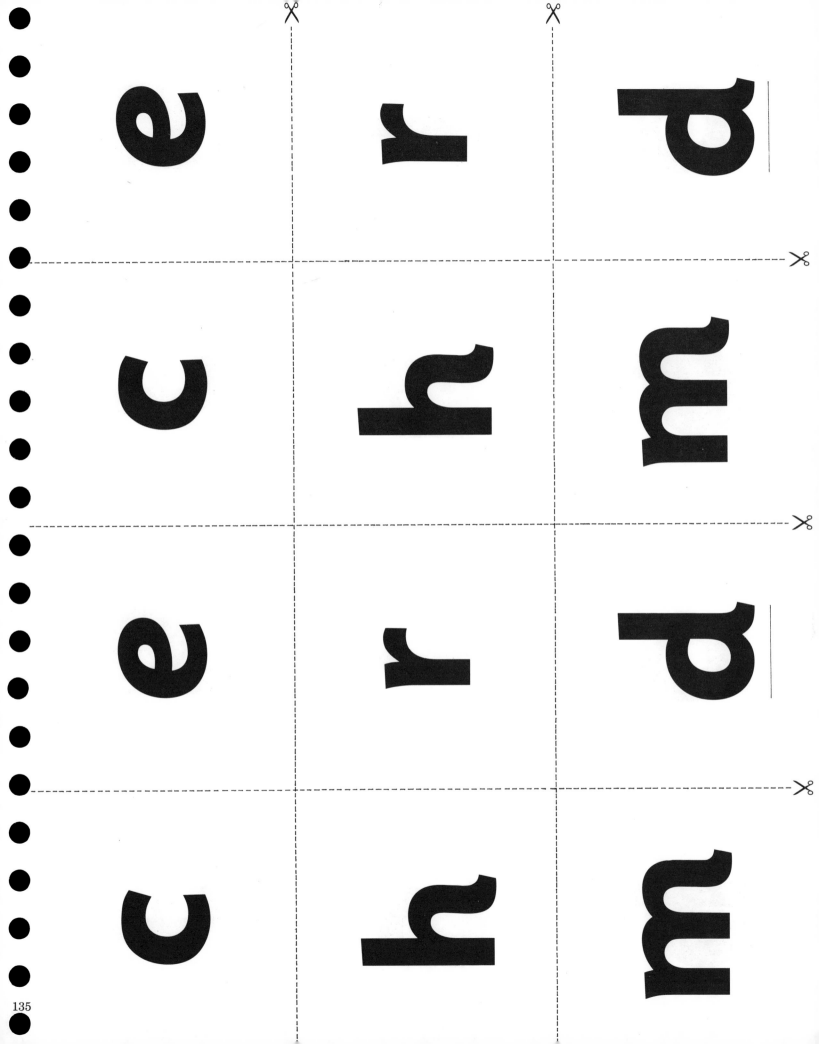

e r d

c h m

e r d

c h m

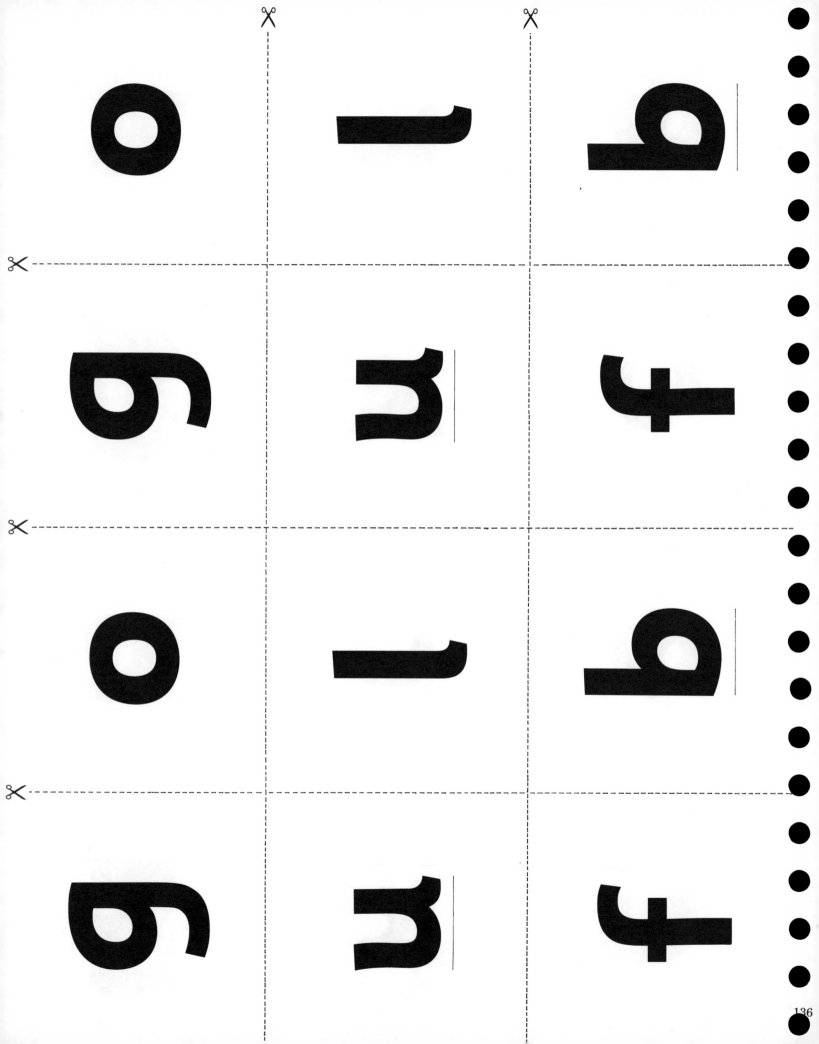

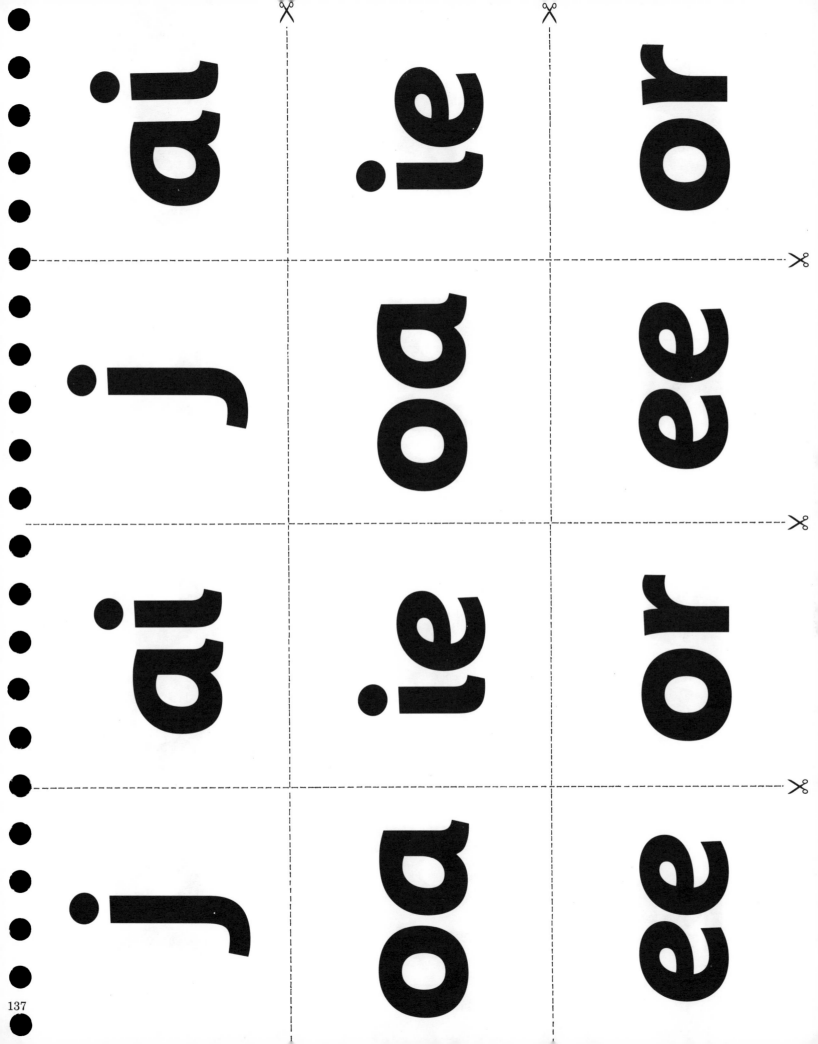

ai    ie    or

j    oa    ee

ai    ie    or

j    oa    ee

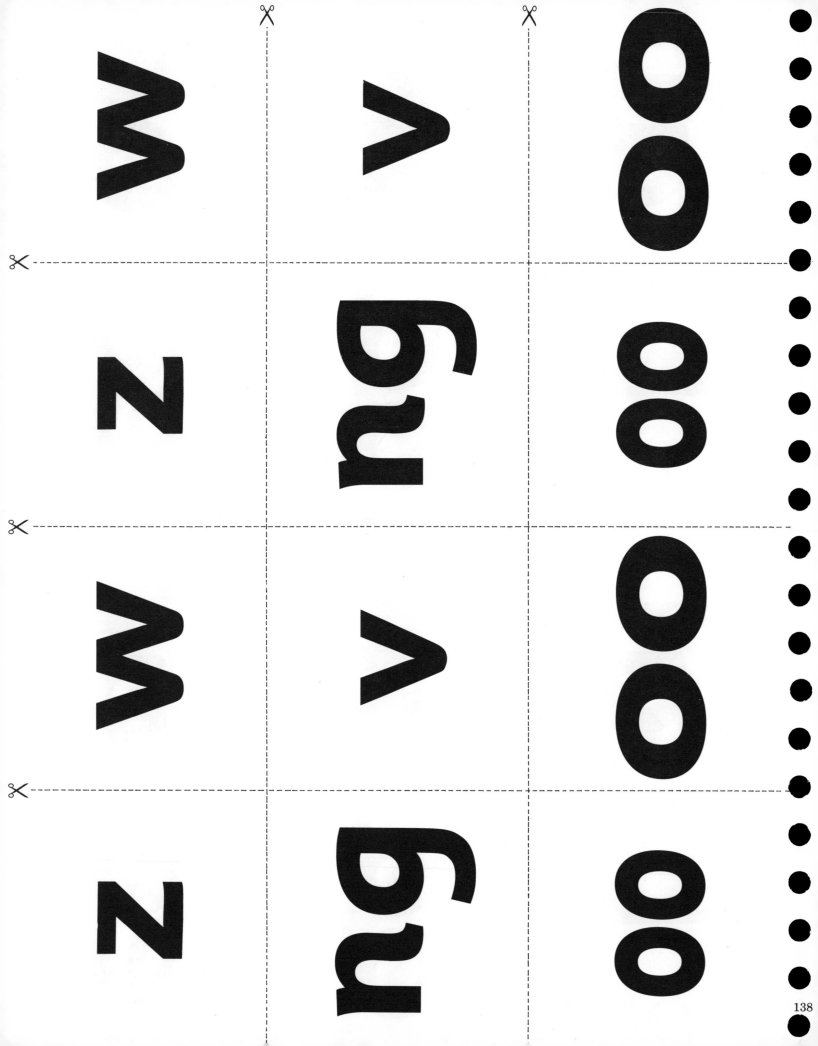

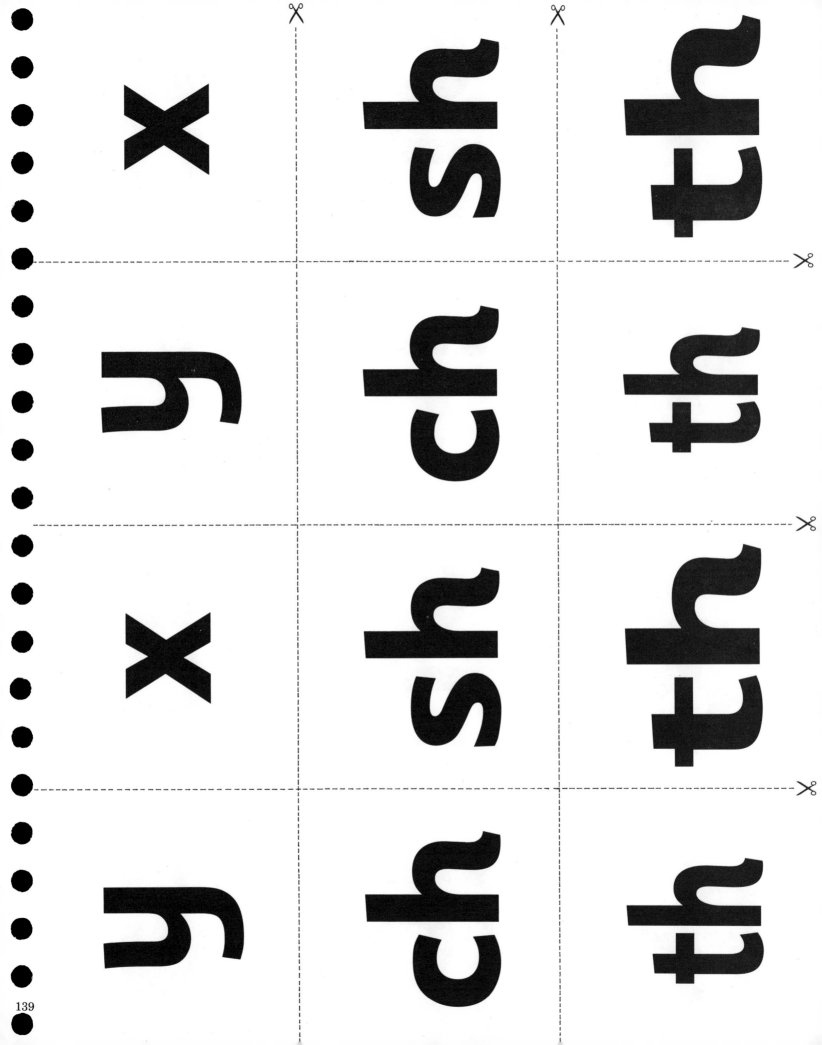

x

y

x

y

sh

ch

sh

ch

th

th

th

th

ou

ue

ar

qu

oi

er

ou

ue

ar

qu

oi

er

# *Word Box Sheets*

The Word Box Sheets have been graded to progress from the very simple, using the earliest learned sounds, to more complex multi-syllabic words. Their main function is to achieve greater fluency and to provide practice in blending letters before the introduction of readers.

They should be introduced when children can hear words they have sounded out by themselves and in this way a sense of achievement is experienced by all children. These groups of words provide the stepping stones between letters, words and books.

Once the children have reached this stage, they are eager to practice their skills at home. Parental co-operation is important because, with their help, the children progress through this stage at maximum speed. Most children can manage a new group of words each night.

Inevitably some children will be able to read some words without saying the sounds. This is to be encouraged but should not be required. The goal is to develop the skill of sounding out words rather than developing visual memory.

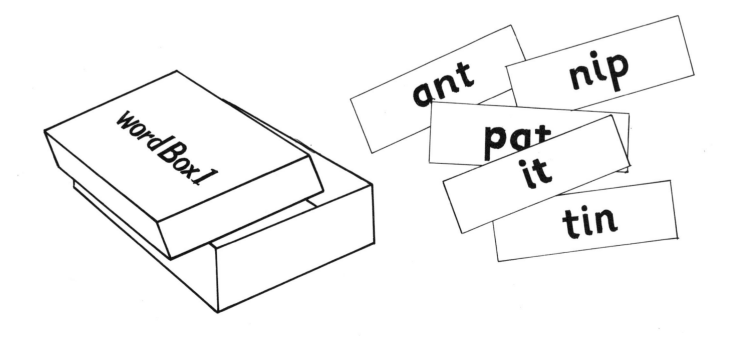

Each Word Box Sheet has the words to cut out and make three Word Boxes:

| Word Box 1 | Word Box 2 | Word Box 3 |
|------------|------------|------------|
| it | pest | hip |
| tin | tap | pet |
| pat | pin | mat |
| nip | is | ran |
| sat | pit | dip |
| as | snap | ham |
| ant | in | map |
| tip | man | rat |
| pan | red | ink |
| sit | dip | rip |

| Word Box 1a | Word Box 2a | Word Box 3a |
|---|---|---|
| nap | egg | nut |
| tan | end | fluff |
| set | ill | lost |
| hill | sack | hog |
| hand | den | tug |
| sand | fist | got |
| men | bin | stuck |
| elf | fed | slug |
| snip | lock | slab |
| ram | hop | fill |

144

| Word Box 4 | Word Box 5 | Word Box 6 |
|---|---|---|
| cat | kiss | drip |
| hen | mist | miss |
| can | best | rock |
| hat | hiss | back |
| neck | test | duck |
| camp | get | pot |
| kick | pig | gas |
| met | log | fit |
| pen | fat | stamp |
| deck | bat | bad |

145

| Word Box 4a | Word Box 5a | Word Box 6a |
|---|---|---|
| cub | rain | or |
| gun | jog | cork |
| flip | coat | see |
| land | jail | seed |
| fun | loaf | sheet |
| band | lie | storm |
| bun | rail | born |
| loft | snail | float |
| run | tree | oak |
| gift | feed | sail |

| Word Box 7 | Word Box 8 | Word Box 9 |
|---|---|---|
| leg | mud | bit |
| rot | from | let |
| up | grill | tub |
| top | spot | lick |
| but | lap | sniff |
| flag | mom | soft |
| brick | fan | frog |
| slip | flat | luck |
| fog | lamp | cup |
| flap | dad | not |

147

| Word Box 7a | Word Box 8a | Word Box 9a |
|---|---|---|
| paid | peep | grip |
| goal | sport | pack |
| soak | creep | grin |
| free | main | swell |
| week | moan | west |
| bleed | speed | peep |
| groan | aim | horn |
| paint | faint | pork |
| toast | vest | sweet |
| tie | well | street |

148

| Word Box 10 | Word Box 11 | Word Box 12 |
| --- | --- | --- |
| pain | keep | wet |
| jet | sleep | zip |
| rain | die | swim |
| jug | for | buzz |
| boat | fork | ring |
| pie | green | long |
| bee | torch | van |
| goat | tail | look |
| nail | road | cling |
| soap | weed | swing |

| Word Box 10a | Word Box 11a | Word Box 12a |
|---|---|---|
| ox | chop | such |
| teeth | spoon | chimp |
| sheep | hang | cash |
| chin | chuck | this |
| yak | sixth | shot |
| wax | dish | them |
| much | chill | rush |
| song | shop | then |
| bring | thump | cloth |
| fool | cash | chain |

| Word Box 13 | Word Box 14 | Word Box 15 |
|---|---|---|
| bang | yes | box |
| string | six | that |
| fizz | fox | with |
| good | lunch | thin |
| zoo | chick | moth |
| roof | shed | thank |
| swam | flash | rich |
| tooth | wish | shut |
| wool | chest | ship |
| strong | shock | think |

151

| Word Box 13a | Word Box 14a | Word Box 15a |
|---|---|---|
| shall | barn | lung |
| pinch | coil | cling |
| fresh | meet | zebra |
| art | foam | will |
| foil | porch | clang |
| round | stork | crook |
| star | three | broom |
| hard | loan | stool |
| summer | coal | hook |
| term | greed | cook |

152

| Word Box 16 | Word Box 17 | Word Box 18 |
|---|---|---|
| yet | loud | quick |
| shelf | quit | out |
| chip | butter | shout |
| crash | bark | queen |
| brush | soil | boil |
| thick | rooster | oil |
| shell | found | due |
| sink | start | park |
| rash | charm | shark |
| fish | toy | litter |

153

| Word Box 16a | Word Box 17a | Word Box 18a |
| --- | --- | --- |
| moo | spill | big |
| sang | spin | bug |
| king | blot | sift |
| fuzz | spend | lad |
| swung | grim | gap |
| wing | gulp | fin |
| moon | spell | frill |
| root | luck | hem |
| wood | grain | grand |
| brand | peck | gruff |

154

*Reproducible Section 5*

# Homework Writing Sheets

Approximately 40% of our words are regular and can be spelled correctly by listening for the sounds and writing the letters that relate to those sounds. Examples of such words are: went, run, left, etc. As this is such a large percentage, it is important for children to practice sounding out and writing these words. The Homework Writing Sheets that follow are designed for this and are a good way of developing independent writing. Most children are ready to start this work towards the end of the first semester and should be able to write a page on their own by the end of the year.

## Homework Writing Book

Each child will need a Homework Writing Book. Prepare each book by stapling together sheets of wide-lined manuscript paper. Reproduce the first of the Homework Writing Sheets, allowing one copy for each child. Write a child's name on each sheet, in the top right-hand corner. Cut off one of the groups of ten words. This goes home in the Homework Writing Book, with the instructions that ask the parents to dictate the words to their child. These instructions are provided on page 165 in this Reproducible Section, in the form of strips.

Most children bring the book back the next day, not because it is required but because they are enthusiastic. Not all the words have to be correct before giving the next group of words, however you should look at the mistakes and go over them with the child. Perhaps he/she hasn't listened for the sounds carefully enough or doesn't know how to write some letters.

The first page of the Homework Writing Sheets has simple three-letter, phonically regular words. The next page has supplementary three-letter words which are useful for children who need more practice. Sheets with four or more letters follow on the same basis. The last four sheets have words with vowels written in different ways.

On page 165 are several copies of instructions for parents, one of which can be sent home with each child with their Homework Writing Sheet.

| | | |
|---|---|---|
| cat | cap | set |
| dog | dot | hit |
| dad | mat | it |
| red | tap | dip |
| top | did | mom |
| six | rot | bet |
| him | sat | yes |
| hat | pet | hut |
| sad | had | zip |
| hot | ham | lap |

| | | |
|---|---|---|
| up | hid | van |
| let | hum | jug |
| rod | gun | in |
| hop | job | on |
| cot | pig | men |
| mud | win | bun |
| bed | not | leg |
| lid | sun | wet |
| bit | web | fun |
| bat | fog | cab |

| | | |
|---|---|---|
| log | big | dug |
| jam | bag | mix |
| rug | ox | fed |
| net | am | bin |
| lip | if | pop |
| tip | cod | bus |
| hug | bud | gas |
| got | gap | fix |
| dig | mug | pod |
| lot | an | nut |
| run | can | rub |
| bad | hen | man |
| get | fit | vet |
| jog | mad | cut |
| bug | ten | pan |
| met | pit | fat |
| lit | fox | map |
| pot | cup | rip |
| us | rat | rob |
| bet | jet | pin |

| | | |
|---|---|---|
| step | list | bump |
| pram | west | hunt |
| damp | just | bent |
| mist | spit | hand |
| lamp | mend | loft |
| test | misty | spin |
| body | jump | band |
| limp | wind | just |
| slip | clip | tent |
| drum | dump | very |

| | | |
|---|---|---|
| chin | film | smash |
| trap | then | wing |
| plum | grin | bench |
| lost | bang | drop |
| hush | cloth | stamp |
| snap | quilt | crust |
| fresh | bulb | from |
| swim | sting | golf |
| long | flat | bunch |
| split | blunt | thing |

| | | |
|---|---|---|
| ship | snip | sand |
| fish | hung | crash |
| stand | wish | that |
| them | bend | this |
| bran | belt | song |
| chip | melt | land |
| shop | lump | quiz |
| thump | went | dish |
| shelf | must | cash |
| pinch | lend | sang |

| | | |
|---|---|---|
| rich | swing | crab |
| with | much | chop |
| chest | frost | swam |
| lunch | spend | shed |
| club | flash | glad |
| best | ring | shut |
| camp | help | ant |
| flag | frog | soft |
| plug | thin | scrub |
| slept | slug | held |

| ai/a-e/ay | ee/ea | ie/i-e/igh/y |
|---|---|---|
| game | bee | pie |
| rain | eat | life |
| date | clean | fry |
| pain | sweet | night |
| stay | weep | high |
| paid | peas | dive |
| lane | leaf | wife |
| wave | sheep | five |
| train | speak | cry |
| day | feed | tie |

| oa/o-e/ow | er/ir/ur | ou/ow |
|---|---|---|
| home | bird | out |
| mole | sister | cow |
| sparrow | burst | clown |
| boat | winter | proud |
| hope | girl | drown |
| bone | burnt | cloud |
| snow | third | shout |
| toast | turnip | down |
| goat | shirt | found |
| show | clever | how |

| ai/a-e/ay | ee/ea | ie/i-e/igh/y |
|---|---|---|
| late | cream | light |
| save | dream | pipe |
| pray | weed | bite |
| paint | feet | fight |
| snail | scream | die |
| came | seeds | ride |
| hay | stream | fly |
| chain | team | shy |
| cave | sweep | shine |
| gate | street | bright |

| oa/o-e/ow | er/ir/ur | ou/ow |
|---|---|---|
| slow | first | mouth |
| those | blister | brown |
| rope | dirt | crowd |
| coach | stir | round |
| pillow | turn | count |
| coat | diver | now |
| stone | thirsty | owl |
| slope | church | loud |
| float | curl | frown |
| stole | later | south |

| oi/oy | short oo | ar |
|-------|---------|-----|
| boy | good | cart |
| oil | hook | start |
| coin | book | jar |
| toy | broom | park |
| soil | wood | car |
| spoil | stood | smart |
| joy | wool | sharp |
| moist | crook | march |
| boil | look | card |
| point | shook | part |

| or/au/aw | c/k/ck | short i/y |
|----------|--------|-----------|
| August | cake | sit |
| jaw | cook | windy |
| saw | duck | tidy |
| fork | luck | bin |
| pork | king | loudly |
| draw | sky | sandy |
| fort | check | clip |
| fault | skate | ink |
| straw | kiss | funny |
| raw | like | sunny |

| oi/oy | long oo | ar |
|---|---|---|
| join | moon | shark |
| joint | spoon | arm |
| enjoy | tooth | yard |
| coil | shoot | scarf |
| foil | food | chart |
| employ | rooster | farm |
| spoilt | boot | barn |
| toil | soon | art |
| appoint | tools | bar |
| cowboy | stool | harsh |

| or/au/aw | c/k/ck | short i/y |
|---|---|---|
| sport | camp | holly |
| shawl | crust | hilly |
| haunt | deck | trip |
| torch | track | silly |
| short | skin | sunny |
| yawn | crush | runny |
| law | chick | mommy |
| forget | stick | daddy |
| north | kick | swim |
| storm | bake | jolly |

## Instructions for Parents — Homework Writing Sheets

In order for children to write phonically regular words by themselves they have to be able to hear the sounds in words, and know how to write the letters for those sounds. Could you help your child practice these skills by dictating these words for him/her to write in the Homework Writing Book.

---

In order for children to write phonically regular words by themselves they have to be able to hear the sounds in words, and know how to write the letters for those sounds. Could you help your child practice these skills by dictating these words for him/her to write in the Homework Writing Book.

---

In order for children to write phonically regular words by themselves they have to be able to hear the sounds in words, and know how to write the letters for those sounds. Could you help your child practice these skills by dictating these words for him/her to write in the Homework Writing Book.

---

In order for children to write phonically regular words by themselves they have to be able to hear the sounds in words, and know how to write the letters for those sounds. Could you help your child practice these skills by dictating these words for him/her to write in the Homework Writing Book.

---

In order for children to write phonically regular words by themselves they have to be able to hear the sounds in words, and know how to write the letters for those sounds. Could you help your child practice these skills by dictating these words for him/her to write in the Homework Writing Book.

---

In order for children to write phonically regular words by themselves they have to be able to hear the sounds in words, and know how to write the letters for those sounds. Could you help your child practice these skills by dictating these words for him/her to write in the Homework Writing Book.

# *Matching Letters, Words and Pictures*

There are eight of these versatile sheets. They can be used in several ways to help the children learn to read and write:

1. a. Make a copy of each page and glue each sheet on card stock. Separate the pictures, letters and words. Lay the first group of pictures out and ask the children to sound out the initial sound and put the appropriate letter or word under the picture.

   b. This can be reversed and the letters put down first and the children match the pictures to the initial letters. After the first three sheets the initial letter is not always applicable and the children may have to listen for a medial or final sound.

   c. Later, the words can be put down and the children have to blend the sounds, read the words and put the appropriate picture underneath. This can also be reversed.

2. Sets of Lotto can be made from the sheets. Copy the gameboards in Reproducible Section 11 (page 207) and glue either the pictures, letters or words on to the boards. Further instructions are also in Reproducible Section 11 (page 204).

3. Pairs Games can be made by pairing the letters to the pictures or the words to the pictures.

4. Independent Writing – lay the pictures out for the children to draw. Then they write the words underneath, by listening for the sounds and writing the letters.

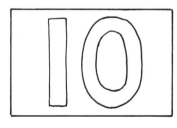  

| i | ink | 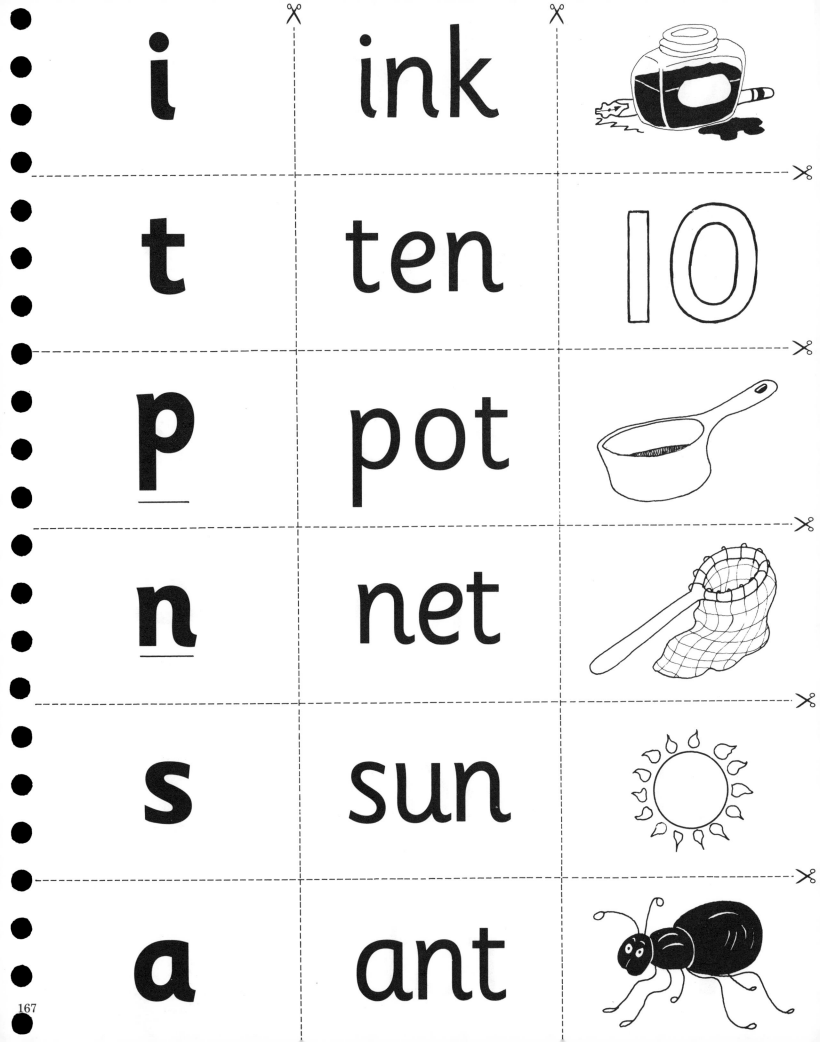 |
| t | ten | |
| p | pot | |
| n | net | |
| s | sun | |
| a | ant | |

167

| d | dog | |
| h | hat | |
| e | egg | |
| c | cup | |
| m | man | |
| r | rat | |

| | | |
|---|---|---|
| g | goat | 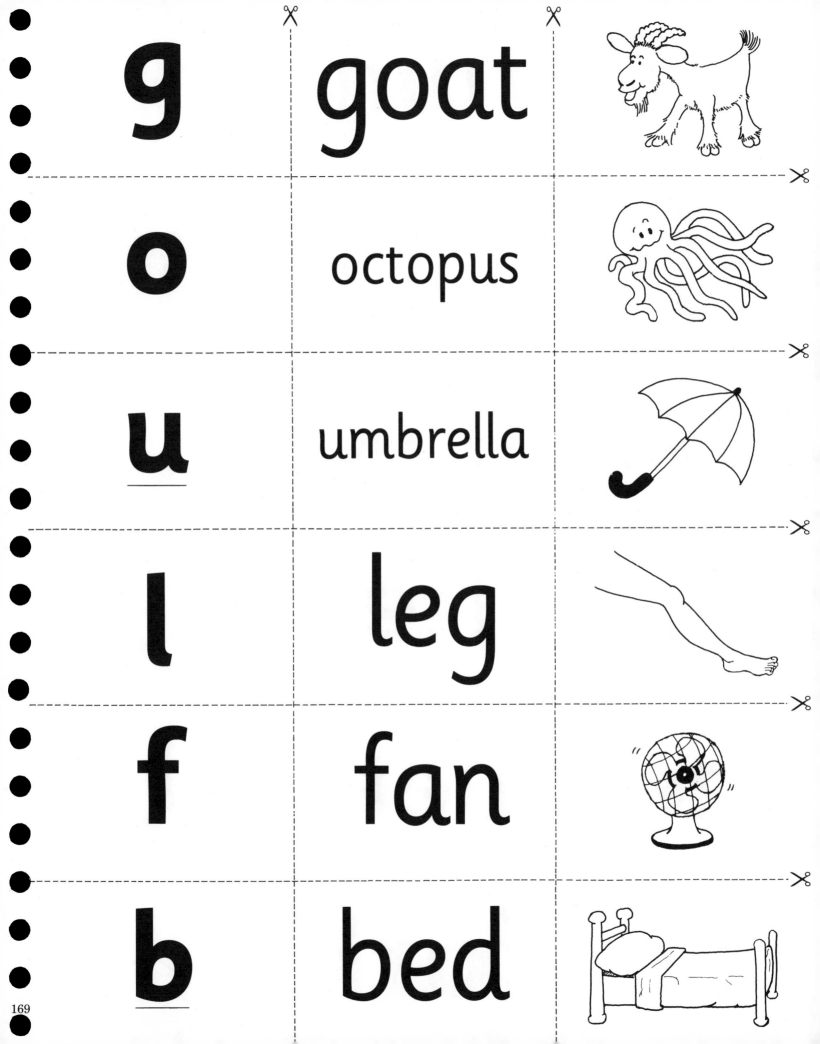 |
| o | octopus | |
| u | umbrella | |
| l | leg | |
| f | fan | |
| b | bed | |

| | | |
|---|---|---|
| **ai** | **rain** | 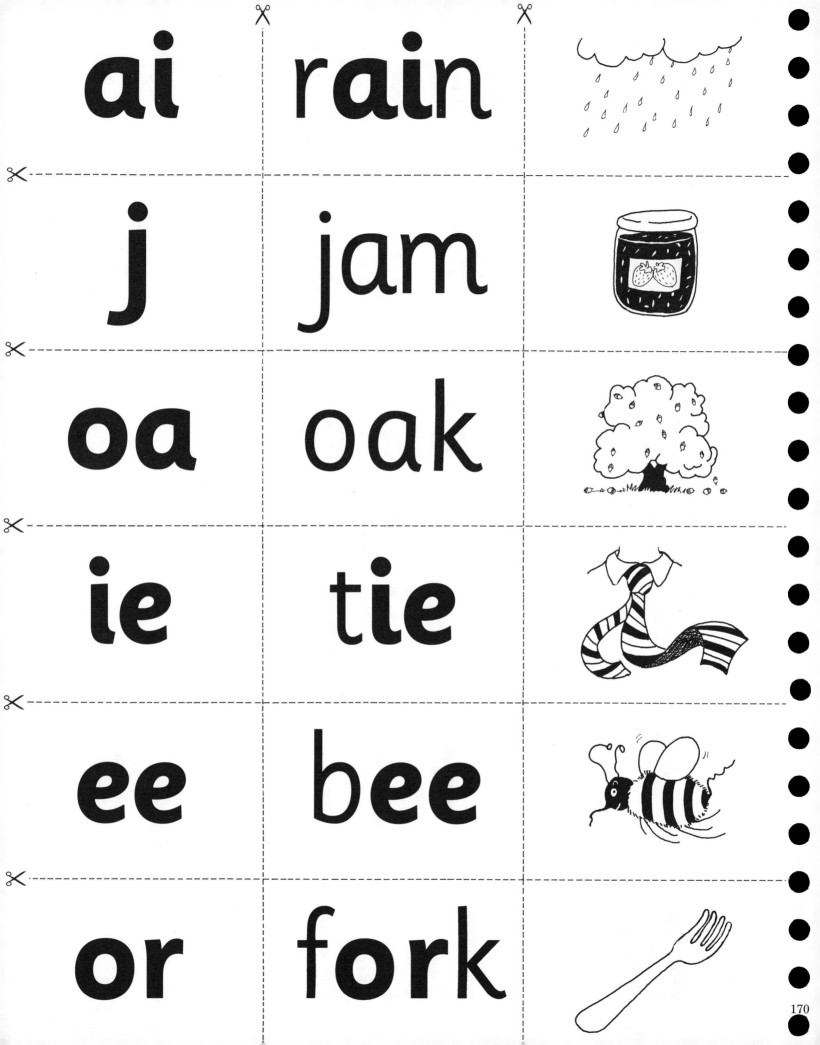 |
| **j** | jam | |
| **oa** | oak | |
| **ie** | **tie** | |
| **ee** | **bee** | |
| **or** | **fork** | |

| z | zebra | |
| w | web | |
| ng | ring | |
| v | van | |
| oo | book | |
| oo | moon | |

| **th** | feather | |
|---|---|---|
| **th** | moth | |
| **y** | yo-yo | |
| **x** | fox | |
| **ch** | chick | |
| **sh** | ship | |

172

| qu | queen | |
| ou | cloud | |
| oi | oil | |
| er | butter | |
| ar | car | |
| ue | cue | |

| k | king | |
| a-e | gate | |
| ea | leaf | |
| i-e | kite | |
| o-e | bone | |
| u-e | cube | |

174

# Letter Clue Pictures

Children who can hear the rhyming part in words, tend to find it easier to read and write. The following sheets help develop auditory skills for hearing rhymes.

Ask children to put the missing letters on the lines, read the words and draw the relevant pictures in the little spaces provided above the words.

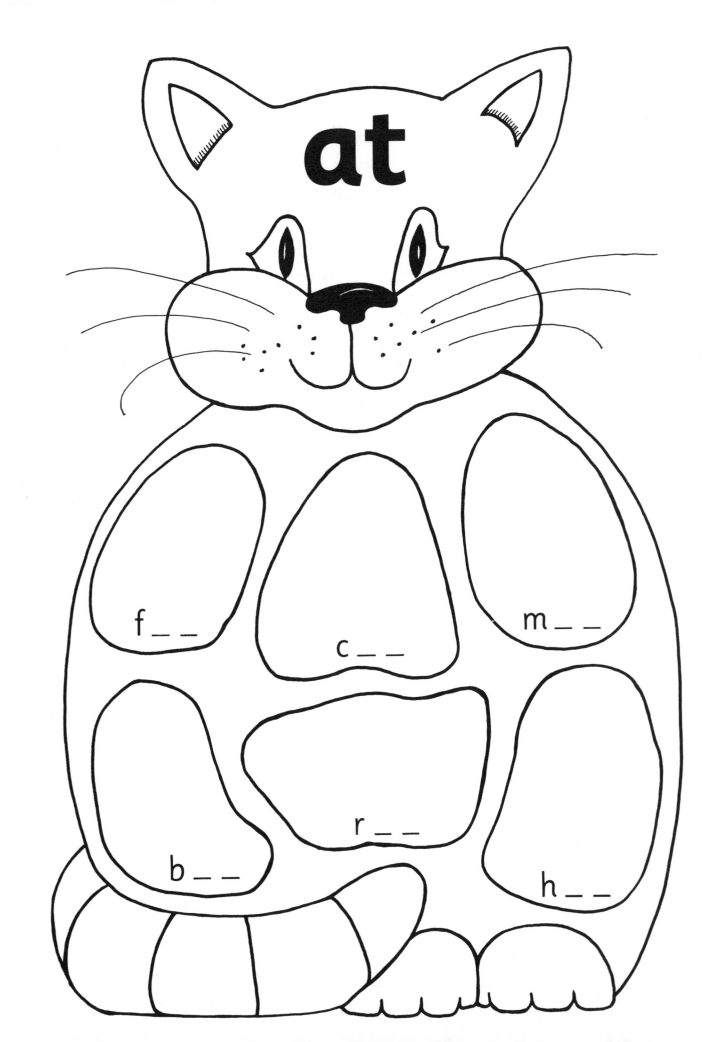

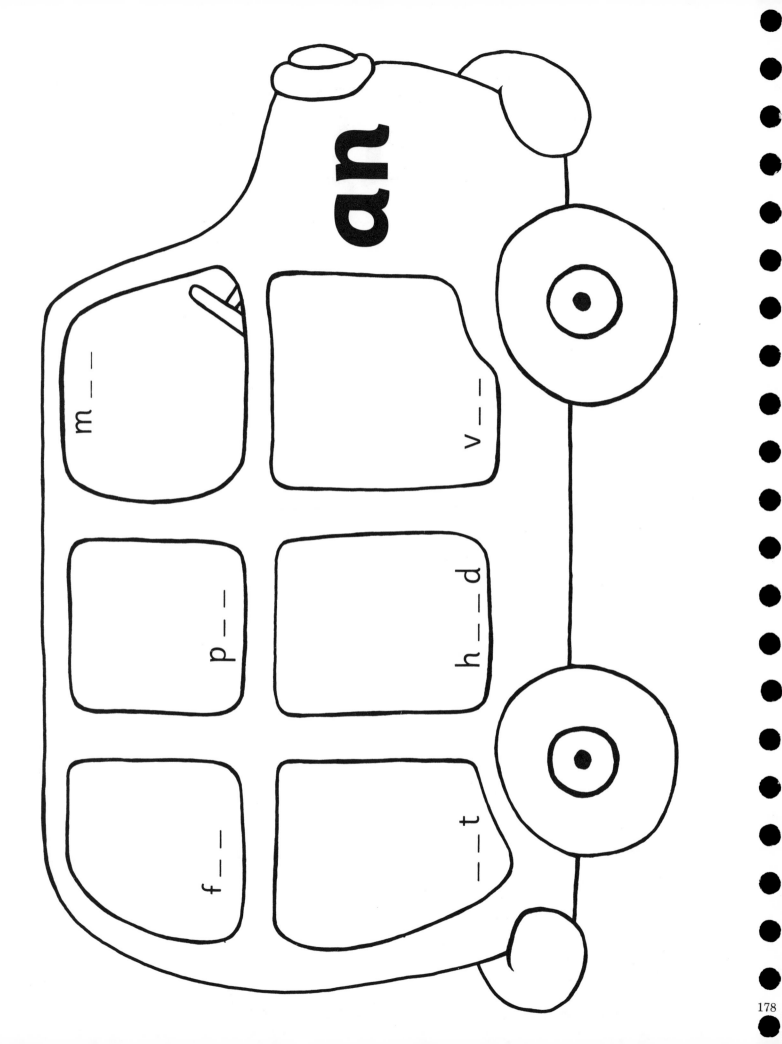

an

m _ _
v _ _
p _ _
h _ _
f _ _
_ _ t

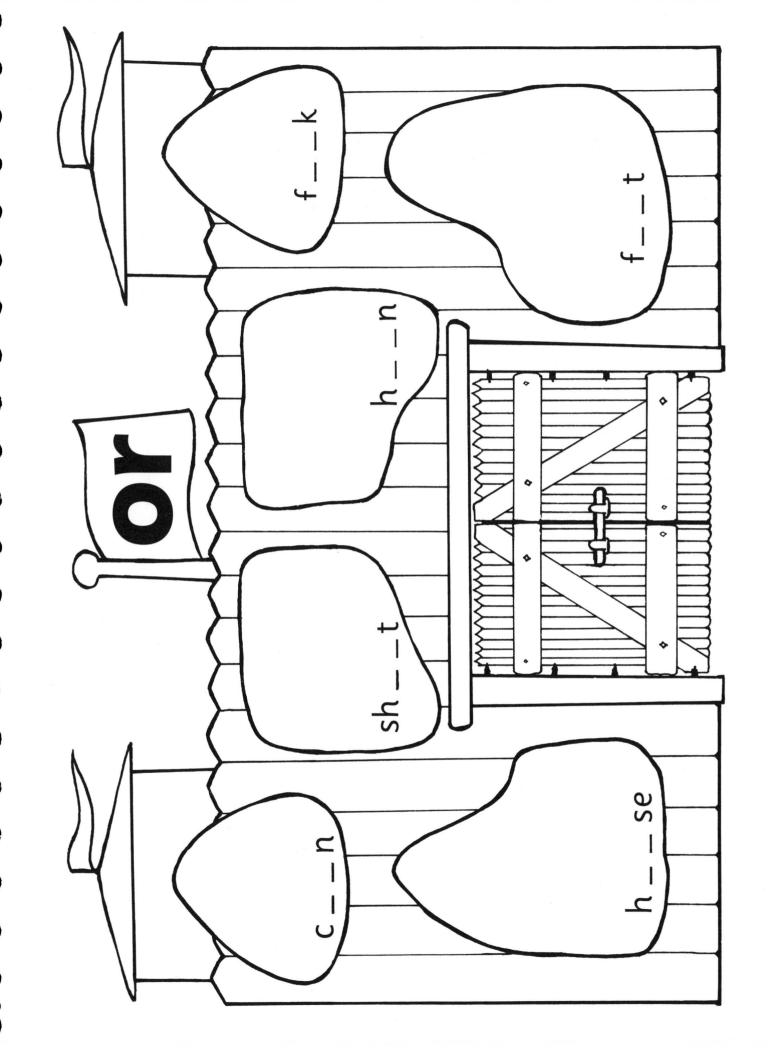

f _ k

f _ _ t

h _ n

**or**

sh _ _ t

c _ _ n

h _ _ se

179

# Missing Sounds

Independent writing, by listening for the sounds and writing the letters, needs to be developed gradually. These progressive worksheets are designed for this purpose.

## Missing Sounds – pages 181-185

This set of sheets has pictures with lines underneath. Ask the children to listen for the sounds and put the letters on the lines. If this is too difficult you could write in some of the letters and leave only one to be filled in.

## Missing Sounds – pages 186-190

This set of sheets has a missing word in a sentence. It is much the same as the first set, except there is a little reading to do as well.

_ _ _ _                    _ _ _ _                    _ _ _ _

_ _ _ _                    _ _ _ _                    _ _ _ _

_ _ _ _                    _ _ _ _

_ _ _ _ _ _ _ _ _ _ _ _ _ _ _ _ _ _

_ _ _ _ _ _ _ _ _ _ _ _ _ _ _ _ _ _

_ _ _ _ _ _ _ _ _ _ _ _ _ _ _ _ _ _

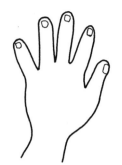

\_ \_ \_ \_ \_ \_ \_ \_ \_ \_ \_ \_

\_ \_ \_ \_ \_ \_ \_ \_ \_ \_ \_ \_

\_ \_ \_ \_ \_ \_ \_ \_ \_ \_ \_ \_

- - - - - - - - - - - -   - - - - - - - - - -   - - - - - - - - - -

 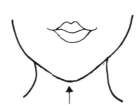 

- - - - - - - - - - - -   - - - - - - - - - -   - - - - - - - - - -

- - - - - - - - - - - -   - - - - - - - - - -

185

I can see a __ __ __.

I can see the __ __ __.

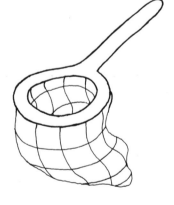

I can see a __ __ __.

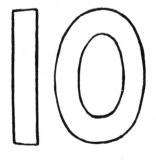

I can see a __ __ __.

**Here is a** __ __ __.

**Here is a** __ __ __.

**Here is a** __ __ __.

**Here is a** __ __ __.

**This is a __ __ __ .**

**This is a __ __ __ __ .**

**This is a __ __ __ .**

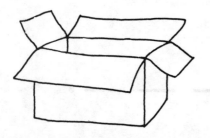

**This is a __ __ __ .**

**The** _ _ _ _ **is green.**

**My** _ _ _ **has got stripes.**

**My** _ _ _ _ _ **has a zipper.**

**The** _ _ _ _ _ _ **has a shell.**

The _ _ _ _ is shining.

I clap with my _ _ _ _ _.

The _ _ _ _ is green.

The _ _ _ _ has a crown.

## Reproducible Section 9

# *String Joining*

There are six of these sheets (pages 192-197) to practice reading by blending the sounds. They can be used in one of two ways:

1.  Copy the sheets and let the children read the words and draw a line to the corresponding pictures.

2.  Turn the sheets into String Cards. These are very popular. Glue the sheets on card stock, color the pictures and laminate. Make holes at the end of each word and the beginning of each picture. Knot laces, preferably brightly colored ones, in the holes by the words. The children then read each word and put the lace through the hole in front of the correct picture.

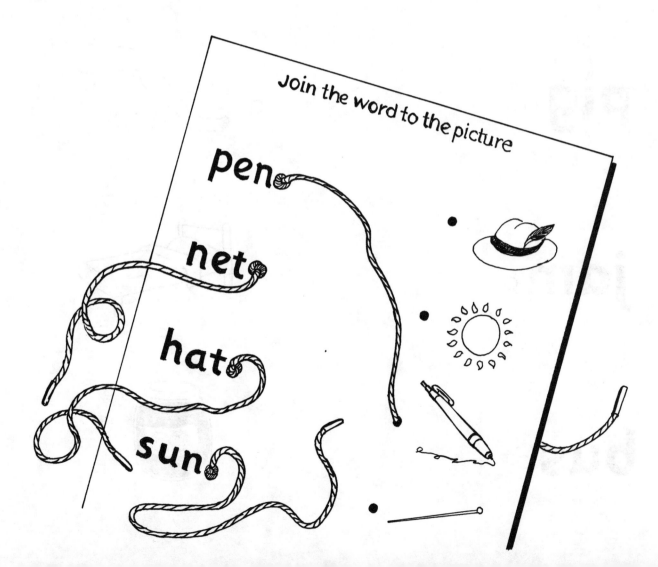

# Join the word to the picture

**bed** ○　　　○

**leg** ○　　　○

**pig** ○　　　○

**jam** ○　　　○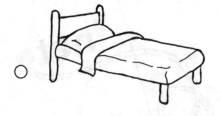

**bus** ○　　　○

192

# Join the word to the picture

pen ○

net ○

hat ○

sun ○

pin ○

○

○

○

○

○

# Join the word to the picture

hen ○

○

can ○

○

dog ○

○

rug ○

○

cup ○

○

# Join the word to the picture

cat ○

○

van ○

○

fan ○

○

ant ○

○

fox ○

○

# Join the word to the picture

**flag** ○      ○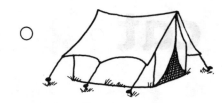

**tent** ○      ○

**drum** ○      ○

**hand** ○      ○

**nest** ○      ○

# Join the word to the picture

**crab** ○  ○

**twig** ○  ○

**crib** ○  ○

**belt** ○  ○

**pond** ○ 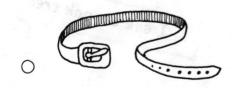 ○

## Reproducible Section 10

# Sentence Sticking

These four sheets (pages 199-202) are very popular because little children love cutting and gluing.

The children cut the sentences off the sheets, read them and glue them under the correct pictures. Then they can color the pictures.

The boat is sailing.

She is running.

I see a bunch of flowers.

This sock is long

The sun is hot.

The soap is in the dish.

199

A duck swims on the pond

It is raining.

The apple pie is hot.

I clap my hands.

The pig is fat.

I see the moon and stars.

The dog is spotty.

We had fries for dinner.

I paint with a brush.

The bell is ringing.

I see an oak tree

I sleep in a bed.

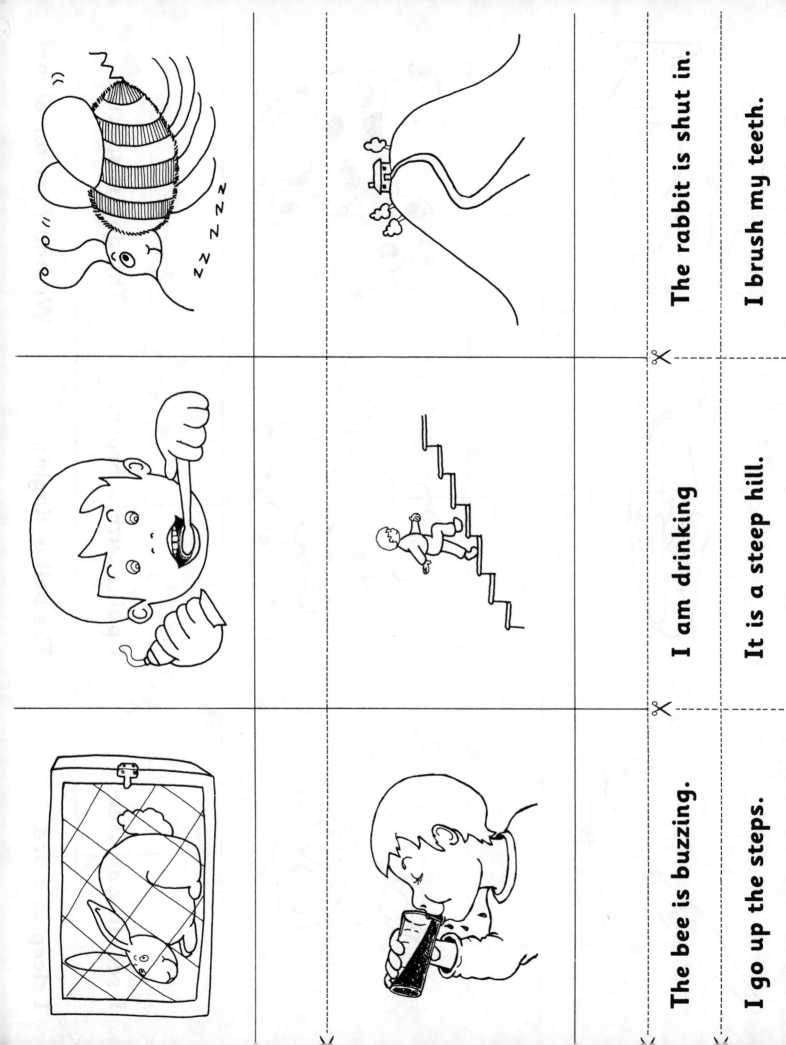

The rabbit is shut in.

I brush my teeth.

I am drinking

It is a steep hill.

The bee is buzzing.

I go up the steps.

# *Letter Games*

Playing games with children is very worthwhile. The children learn to co-operate with each other and develop a sense of right and wrong. It is also a very effective way of learning.

In the classroom it is difficult to play games, unless there is plenty of adult help available. It is much better to encourage parents to play games with their children. This not only helps their children learn to read and write but makes for stronger family bonds. The letter games are designed to help children become fluent at reading and writing as quickly as possible.

The games provided are:

> Pairs Games
> Lotto
> Four Reading Games (each with a track to follow)

## Pairs Games

The Pairs Games are very useful for developing memory and reasoning. The children can also learn a great deal as they play. Suggested activities are:

1. To develop fluency in saying the sounds of letters, the parents can be given the Sound Book Sheets pages 133-140, when the sounds have already been taught. They can be encouraged to glue the sheets on card stock, cut out the letters, then lay the letters, face down. As the children turn the cards over, they must say the sounds.

2. Teachers can play the Pairs Game a few times with the class or with a group of children to show them how to play. The Sound Book Sheets in Reproducible Section 3 have two of each letter sounds for this purpose. For the children who get no help at home, these games can be played with a teacher's aide in school, or a child who knows the sounds. Parents notes for using these sheets to play Pairs Games are included in this Reproducible Section.

3. The Matching Letters, Words and Pictures Sheets (Reproducible Section 6) can be turned into Pairs Games. The pictures can be paired with either the letters or the words.

## Lotto Games

To make the Lotto game boards, reproduce the Lotto Board in this section, if possible on card stock. One copy can make 2 Lotto Boards. Then copy the Matching Letters, Words and Pictures (Reproducible Section 6) and glue the pictures on the white spaces on the boards. Protect the boards by laminating them. Then mount the matching words for these pictures on card stock and cut them up so that you have a pack of words. Notes for Parents explaining how to play Lotto have been included in this section.

You can vary the game by using pictures and initial letters, or words and initial letters instead of just pictures and words.

## Reading Games

There are four games with a track to follow. Each game requires some reading, starting with simple three-letter words and progressing to multi-syllabic words. It is another way of giving the children practice in blending sounds to read words. Notes for Parents about playing the Reading Games have been included.

# *Parents Notes – Pairs Sheets*

These sheets of letters can be used in several ways. Each sheet has two of each letter on it. By playing with them, you can help your child to become fluent at saying the sounds that go with letters.

Children sometimes have a resistance to their parents being like the teachers. Therefore, the more casual the teaching is, through games and activities, the more the children like it.

## Activity 1 – Pairs Game

Glue the sheet on card stock – a side of a cereal box will do. Cut up the letters and turn them face down. The first person to start, turns over two of the letters. As they do this, they say the sounds. If the letters are the same, they keep them and take another turn. When they are not the same, they are returned and the next person takes a turn. The person to get the most pairs is the winner. Gradually the children realize that it helps to remember where the letters are after they have been turned over. It is important to say the sound every time each letter is revealed. The aim of the game is to get the children fluent at saying the correct letter sounds.

## Activity 2 – Reading Words

Pick out letters that make a word, eg: pin, pot, sit, sat, pat, pan, etc. Ask your child to sound it out and read the word. Be sure to use regular words that can be sounded out. Avoid words like one, only, put, etc. If your child is having difficulty doing this do it together. With practice it eventually becomes easy for all children

## Activity 3 – Building Words

In this activity, you are to ask your child to pick out the letters in a word. Say a simple word such as 'sit', ask him/her to listen for the sounds in that word and pick out the correct letters. In the beginning, you may have to do it together, but as he or she gets more confident, he/she can do it alone. Encourage your child to lay down the letters in the correct left to right order and see if he/she can read it as well. Your child has been taught how to hear the sounds in words and identify them. Some children find this difficult at first and just cannot hear them. If this is the case, with your child it is better to delay this activity.

## Parents Notes – Lotto

Two people can play the Lotto Game and each player has a game board. The cards with words (or letters) need to be shuffled and placed face down. Players take turns picking up a card and reading it. The word (or letter) is put on the corresponding picture on that player's game board, or else returned to the bottom of the deck of cards. The winner is the first player to cover all the pictures on his/her game board.

Two people can play the Lotto Game and each player has a game board. The cards with words (or letters) need to be shuffled and placed face down. Players take turns picking up a card and reading it. The word (or letter) is put on the corresponding picture on that player's game board, or else returned to the bottom of the deck of cards. The winner is the first player to cover all the pictures on his/her game board.

Two people can play the Lotto Game and each player has a game board. The cards with words (or letters) need to be shuffled and placed face down. Players take turns picking up a card and reading it. The word (or letter) is put on the corresponding picture on that player's game board, or else returned to the bottom of the deck of cards. The winner is the first player to cover all the pictures on his/her game board.

Two people can play the Lotto Game and each player has a game board. The cards with words (or letters) need to be shuffled and placed face down. Players take turns picking up a card and reading it. The word (or letter) is put on the corresponding picture on that player's game board, or else returned to the bottom of the deck of cards. The winner is the first player to cover all the pictures on his/her game board.

Two people can play the Lotto Game and each player has a game board. The cards with words (or letters) need to be shuffled and placed face down. Players take turns picking up a card and reading it. The word (or letter) is put on the corresponding picture on that player's game board, or else returned to the bottom of the deck of cards. The winner is the first player to cover all the pictures on his/her game board.

# *Parents Notes – Reading Games*

A die is needed to play the games. It is better to restrict the numbers on the die to 1, 2 and 3. Cover the numbers 4, 5 and 6 and write 1, 2 and 3 on them. Counters are also needed for each player.

Put the counters on the 'Start'. Each player takes a turn to throw the die and move along. When a player lands on a word, he/she reads it. If it is correct then he/she moves on one space and if it is not read correctly then the player goes back one space. The first person to reach 'Finish', is the winner. Players do not need to throw an exact number to finish.

A die is needed to play the games. It is better to restrict the numbers on the die to 1, 2 and 3. Cover the numbers 4, 5 and 6 and write 1, 2 and 3 on them. Counters are also needed for each player.

Put the counters on the 'Start'. Each player takes a turn to throw the die and move along. When a player lands on a word, he/she reads it. If it is correct then he/she moves on one space and if it is not read correctly then the player goes back one space. The first person to reach 'Finish', is the winner. Players do not need to throw an exact number to finish.

A die is needed to play the games. It is better to restrict the numbers on the die to 1, 2 and 3. Cover the numbers 4, 5 and 6 and write 1, 2 and 3 on them. Counters are also needed for each player.

Put the counters on the 'Start'. Each player takes a turn to throw the die and move along. When a player lands on a word, he/she reads it. If it is correct then he/she moves on one space and if it is not read correctly then the player goes back one space. The first person to reach 'Finish', is the winner. Players do not need to throw an exact number to finish.

A die is needed to play the games. It is better to restrict the numbers on the die to 1, 2 and 3. Cover the numbers 4, 5 and 6 and write 1, 2 and 3 on them. Counters are also needed for each player.

Put the counters on the 'Start'. Each player takes a turn to throw the die and move along. When a player lands on a word, he/she reads it. If it is correct then he/she moves on one space and if it is not read correctly then the player goes back one space. The first person to reach 'Finish', is the winner. Players do not need to throw an exact number to finish.

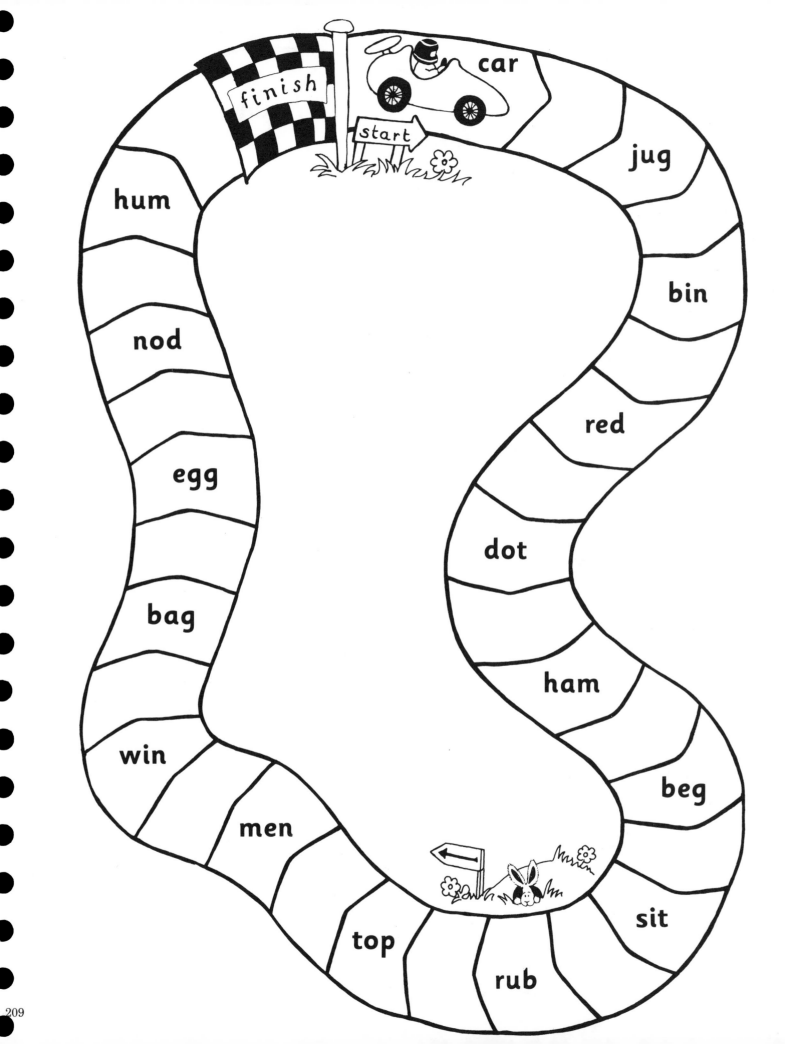

finish

start

car

jug

bin

red

dot

ham

beg

sit

rub

top

men

win

bag

egg

nod

hum

209

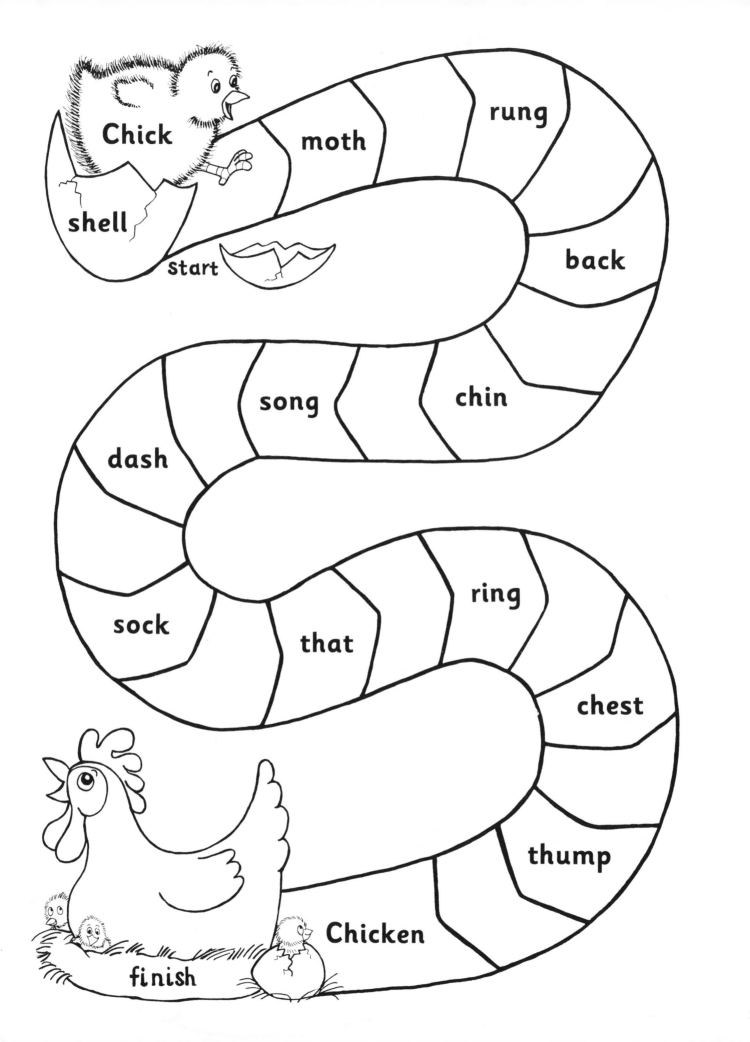

Chick

moth

rung

shell

Start

back

song

chin

dash

sock

ring

that

chest

thump

Chicken

finish

210

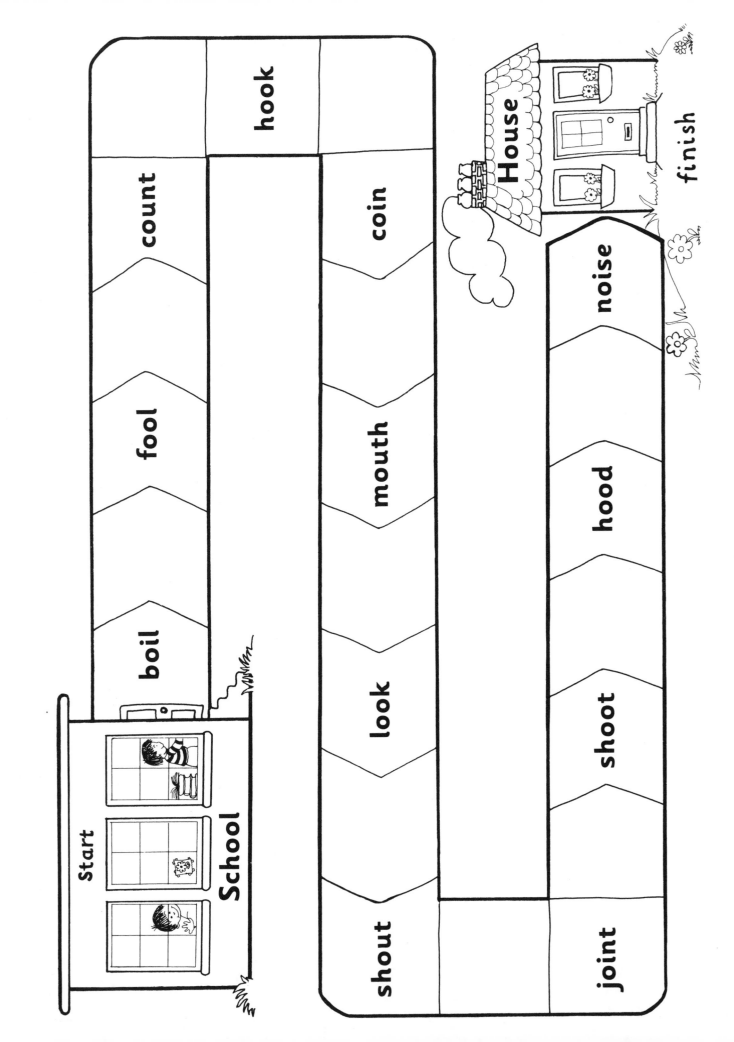

Start

School

hook

count

fool

boil

coin

mouth

look

shout

House

finish

noise

hood

shoot

joint

211

# Award Certificate

Congratulations to _____ for

successfully completing the *Jolly* **Phonics** program

Date _____

Signed by _____

GOOD WORK

*Reproducible Section 12*

# Information for Parents

It is useful to have information that can be given to parents. Included in this section:

# Information for Parents

Learning to read and write fluently is vital if children are going to get maximum value from their education and fulfil their true potential. It is important that reading and writing are mastered as soon as possible for without this ability it is difficult for children to cope with mathematics, science and other subjects.

Your child will be taught to read by a phonic approach that is highly structured. That means he/she will be taught all the sounds that letters make and how to blend them to read unknown words.

For each of the 42 letter sounds, there is an action for the children to do. This helps them to remember the letter sounds and makes it an enjoyable activity. Your support at this stage is invaluable. If you join in with them, you can help your child become really fluent at saying the sounds when he/she sees the letters. As the letters are taught they are glued in a 'Sound Book' which will be brought home regularly. If you go through the book, with your child, he/she will find it easier to remember the sounds. A 'Pairs Game' will also be sent home with instructions for play. Children love playing games and by playing this one your child's fluency at saying the sounds will increase.

Knowing the letter sounds well is not enough. The children need to be able to blend them. They must be able to run the letter sounds together in such a way that they make the word. If you ask your child to say the first sound of a word loudly and quickly whisper the rest, it is easier for them to hear the word. Some children can do this straight away and others take longer. To give your child practice, he/she will bring home boxes of words. You can listen to him/her blending the sounds to read the words and then send the box back to school.

Once your child has been through the boxes of words and is reasonably fluent at blending, he/she will bring home reading books. It will help if you listen to him/her reading aloud. When he/she comes to unknown words ask him/her to try blending the sounds and see if your child can sound out the word. Some words are so irregular that it is impossible to deduce them and you will have to tell your child what that word is. After a while, it is best if they can do the sounding out silently.

Being able to read the words easily is necessary, but it is also important that children understand what they have read. You can help by talking about the story with your child.

If children are going to be able to write by themselves at an early age, they need to be able to hear the sounds in words and write the letters for those sounds. They will be taught to do this. When they are ready, they will bring home a list of words to practice this new writing skill. These words are for you to dictate while your child listens for the sounds in the words that you say and writes down the letters for those sounds in their 'Homework Writing Book'. This prepares your child for independent writing. Later on, usually in their second grade, the children will start a spelling program. Your child will bring home words to learn and your help in dictating the words will help your child develop accurate spelling.

All this sounds a great amount of work, however it is not really because it goes in stages and is spread over a long period of time. A little most days is very helpful. Often children are very tired after school and may not be receptive to more activities. It is better to leave it than push too hard. The learning is meant to be done in a relaxed and playful approach. The whole family can join in some games. There is no doubt that effort on your part, at this stage, is well worth it. An early start to reading and writing is invaluable to your child.

# The letters for the 42 Sounds we use in English

There is a Sound Sheet for each of these sounds, though some are combined on one sheet, such as 'c' and 'k', 'ee' and 'or', etc).

| | | |
|---|---|---|
| a | ...... | ant, sand, caravan |
| ai | ...... | aim, aid, drain |
| b | ...... | bat, bend, crab |
| c | ...... | cat, cot, duck |
| d | ...... | dog, dip, sudden |
| e | ...... | egg, end, shed |
| ee | ...... | eel, creep, tree |
| f | ...... | fog, lift, fluff |
| g | ...... | goat, gap, digger |
| h | ...... | hop, hit, hill |
| i | ...... | ink, indian, drink |
| ie | ...... | pie, tie, die |
| j | ...... | jelly, jet, jumper |
| k | ...... | king, kind, kettle |
| l | ...... | leg, lost, shell |
| m | ...... | man, mill, shrimp |
| n | ...... | nut, nip, spin |
| o | ...... | on, dog, spot |
| oa | ...... | oak, oats, boat |
| p | ...... | pig, pet, step |
| q | ...... | queen, quick, quack |
| r | ...... | run, rabbit, barrel |
| s | ...... | sand, sun, twist |
| t | ...... | top, tug, mat |
| u | ...... | up, under, lung |
| ue | ...... | value, argue, cue |
| v | ...... | van, vet, give |
| w | ...... | wind, wet, swim |
| x | ...... | x-ray, ox, flex |
| y | ...... | yell, yes, yellow |
| z | ...... | zoo, zebra, buzz |
| sh | ...... | ship, shop, wish |
| ch | ...... | chop, chick, much |
| th | ...... | this, then, with (voiced th) |
| th | ...... | thin, thick, thimble (unvoiced th) |
| ng | ...... | song, bang, string |
| oo | ...... | look, good, foot (short oo) |
| oo | ...... | moon, spoon, shoot (long oo) |
| ar | ...... | art, arm, start |
| er | ...... | her, stern, sister |
| or | ...... | order, corn, storm |
| oi | ...... | oil, ointment, spoil |
| ou | ...... | out, cloud, found |

# Different ways of writing vowel sounds

1. **Short a**
   cat
   hat
   flag

2. **Short e**
   bed
   pen
   belt

3. **Short i**
   ink
   pig
   swim

4. **Short o**
   dog
   hot
   frog

5. **Short u**
   bus
   hut
   bulb

6. **Long a**

   | ai | a-e | ay |
   |------|-------|------|
   | rain | date | day |
   | waist | plate | stay |
   | drain | flame | play |

7. **Long e**

   | ee | ea |
   |--------|-------|
   | seed | seat |
   | bleed | cream |
   | street | read |

8. **Long i**

   | ie | i-e | igh | y |
   |-----|------|--------|-----|
   | pie | pipe | night | my |
   | tie | line | fight | fly |
   | die | shine | bright | cry |

9. **Long o**

   | oa | o-e | ow |
   |-------|-------|--------|
   | boat | bone | snow |
   | goat | close | slow |
   | float | smoke | pillow |

217

| 10. | **Long u** | | |
|-----|-----------|--------|--------|
| | ue | u-e | ew |
| | value | cube | few |
| | argue | cute | skew |
| | barbecue | mule | new |

| 11. | **Short oo** | u |
|-----|-------------|--------|
| | book | put |
| | foot | push |
| | shook | pudding |

| 12. | **Long oo** | ue | ew | u-e |
|-----|------------|------|------|------|
| | moon | glue | blew | June |
| | fool | blue | flew | rude |
| | shoot | true | brew | |

| 13. | **The 'ar' sound** | |
|-----|-------------------|--------|
| | ar | a |
| | car | father |
| | arm | ma |
| | star | palm |

| 14. | **The 'er' sound** | | | |
|-----|-------------------|--------|--------|----------|
| | er | ir | ur | e |
| | supper | bird | turn | tunnel |
| | sister | shirt | burn | squirrel |
| | blister | third | purse | garden |

| 15. | **The 'or' sound** | | | |
|-----|-------------------|--------|--------|--------|
| | or | au | aw | al |
| | fork | August | claw | talk |
| | port | pause | saw | walk |
| | storm | fraud | shawl | chalk |

| 16. | **The 'oi' sound** | |
|-----|-------------------|--------|
| | oi | oy |
| | oil | boy |
| | coin | toy |
| | spoil | enjoy |

| 17. | **The 'ou' sound** | |
|-----|-------------------|--------|
| | ou | ow |
| | loud | cow |
| | mouse | clown |
| | cloud | brown |

The two forms of **the 'ng' sound** are useful to know:

| ng | nk |
|------|--------|
| sing | ink |
| bang | blink |
| lung | drunk |